YALE ROMANIC STUDIES, SECOND SERIES 13

ANOUILH

A STUDY IN THEATRICS

BY JOHN HARVEY

NEW HAVEN AND LONDON, YALE UNIVERSITY PRESS, 1964

842.914

H 26 a

63860

November, 1968

Contents

Preface

In April 1932 Pierre Fresnay starred in *L'Hermine,* and the career of a precocious playwright from Bordeaux was launched. Critics hailed in Jean Anouilh a promising avant-garde talent, but his first play, it must be admitted, was little more than a traditional well-made melodrama. By May, *L'Hermine* had lost all its luster, and after only thirty-seven performances it disappeared from the boards. For five years the dramatist was unable to match even this first *succès d'estime. La Mandarine,* written when he was nineteen, folded within two weeks in 1933, and *Y'Avait un Prisonnier,* performed a few years later, fared only slightly better. Metro-Goldwyn-Mayer was impressed by the latter piece, however, and the sale of the film rights brought young Anouilh his first taste of financial independence.

Triumph came in 1937, when the Pitoëffs performed *Le Voyageur sans bagage.* Vaguely patterned after Giraudoux's first play, *Siegfried,* the work aroused a number of comparisons between the two dramatists. It was clear that Anouilh had already transcended his avant-garde status; the critics were now situating him somewhere between—though far beneath—the fanciful Giraudoux and the more an-

guished Salacrou. When Ludmilla Pitoëff gave a searing interpretation of *La Sauvage* a year later, this
impression was confirmed.

Back in 1932 Anouilh had tried to compose a boulevard play, but widely overshooting his mark, he found
himself the father of a freakish comedy-ballet that was
to be shunned for years by Parisian producers. Not
until 1938, when André Barsacq perceived its merits,
was a production attempted. *Le Bal des voleurs* was
an instant success, and has since proved to be one of
the playwright's most endearing and enduring pieces.
Working intimately with Anouilh, Barsacq then went
on to stage the other two "pièces roses"—the pink or
happy plays—*Léocadia* and *Le Rendez-vous de Senlis*.
On the eve of World War II these escapist comedies
were immensely popular, and their author found himself branded a spinner of fantasy—a pink fantasy rid-
dled with the black strands of despair.

During the Occupation, in February 1944, Barsacq
staged Anouilh's greatest single success, *Antigone,*
starring the playwright's wife, Monelle Valentin. For
645 consecutive performances Frenchmen crowded
into the Atelier Theatre, often without electricity, to
see Antigone confront Créon in the narrow patch of
light falling from the stage's skylight. And for once,
Anouilh's bleak theme—the preference of death to
compromise—seemed terribly immediate to his audience. But it was not overly clear: to some observers the
author was championing gauleiter Créon at the expense of his foolishly idealistic heroine. Ambiguity,
which in more normal times may enrich a work of art,
now undermined a writer's position. Besides, during
this same period, Jean-Paul Sartre was turning out far

less ambiguous dramas. Although *Les Mouches,* a year earlier, and *Huis Clos,* to open a few months hence, were no match for *Antigone* in popularity, their content was more novel and their impact on the intelligentsia more compelling and lasting. At the Liberation, then, Anouilh was still considered more of a creator of theatrical fantasy than an intellectual of probing depth.

After the war, Jean Anouilh ventured only twice more into the world of black. *Roméo et Jeannette* in 1946 had a cool reception and owed its respectable run mainly to the comic relief of its minor characters, upon whose entrances listless audiences invariably snapped to life. *Médée,* last of the labeled "pièces noires," or black plays, had to wait seven years for a production which, even then, miscarried. In the intervening years a distinct change developed in Anouilh's theatre. As the more discerning critics had already warned him, his despair was a blind alley: metaphysical rather than psychological or social in nature, its variations were limited, and the artist was inevitably reduced to repeating himself. Henceforth Anouilh was to mine the comic vein, and henceforth his plays were to become increasingly popular. *L'Invitation au château,* a virtual parody of his previous pieces, danced on for almost a year; on its heels came several more hits: *Ardèle, La Répétition, Colombe*—the latter running for 458 performances.

Inevitably, a dramatist writes one play, his director interprets another, the actors perform a third, and the public sees a fourth and altogether different one. In 1948 Anouilh changed directors: he allied himself with Roland Piétri, whose interpretations were more in accord with his own visions. He also began working with a limited, well-trained, and congenial team of actors. And his public continued to grow. It grew so large, in fact, that as *La Répétition* and *Colombe* together dominated the 1950–51 season, critics began wondering if he was not, after all, something of a boulevard playwright. Certainly he was now attracting a boulevard public, having gravitated to the pole furthermost from the avant-garde. On the other hand, just a glance at the "new" avant-garde (it was Anouilh himself who once scoffed that nothing changes less than the avant-garde) revealed how traditional his own dramaturgy had always been.

Throughout the 1950s Sartre and Camus, though far from brilliant craftsmen, maintained their hegemony before the intellectuals of the theatre world. *L'Hurluberlu,* for example, may have been one of the biggest box-office hits of the 1958–59 season, but Camus' adaptation of *Les Possédés,* opening a week before Anouilh's comedy, was truly the intellectual event of the season. The following winter *Becket ou l'honneur de Dieu* drew a storm of praise from the critics, but once again, Sartre's *Les Séquestrés d'Altona,* opening a week earlier, justly claimed the spotlight as the year's most provocative and profound drama. Meanwhile, the younger intellectuals were busy hailing the latest works of their idols: Ionesco's *Le Tueur sans gages* and *Rhinocéros,* Genet's *Les Nègres* and *Le Balcon,* and Beckett's *Krapp's Last Tape.*

Thus has Anouilh's career entered its most recent phase. Giraudoux and his nearly indispensable interpreter, Louis Jouvet, have both died; Salacrou, after a string of failures, has fallen squarely into the background; the great epoch of existentialism is a matter of history; Camus has died; so that current rivals are Ionesco, Beckett, and Genet. After thirty years of writing and nearly that many original Paris productions, Jean Anouilh remains one of the more esteemed, popular, and productive of French playwrights. Although a few of his pieces, such as *L'Invitation au château* or *Antigone*, have already enjoyed a measure of international success and frequent, happy revivals in France, it is still too early to say whether any of them is a masterpiece. Indeed, if Anouilh is to survive, it is more likely that it will be on the basis of his complete works, free of the dazzle (and tarnish) of easy trickery, works not grounded in contemporary references, works of traditional or "pure" theatre. Pure theatre is another way of saying pure form; and mere form, no matter how perfect, is no key to immortality. Even those who most admire Anouilh's technical virtuosity are often the least impressed by the content of his plays—thin, repetitive, despairing, and infantile, they say. Whether Anouilh has in fact had as many ideas as Racine or Molière, and whether his views on society and man are more pessimistic or less pessimistic than is warranted, will not concern us here. Rather, it is our intention to explore the skills that have enabled Anouilh to give stunning dramatic form to whatever has obsessed his mind and heart.

I am most grateful to MM. Jean-Denis Malclès, Christian Lude, and Jean-Louis Roncoroni for their valuable assistance, and to Mme. Claude Chevalley at the Comédie-Française and Mlle. E. Ducoin at the Bibliothèque des Régisseurs for their permission to consult unpublished manuscripts. I am especially indebted to Jacques Guicharnaud of Yale University for his encouragement and judicious suggestions during the preparation of the manuscript.

J.H.

Northampton, Massachusetts
February 1964

Abbreviations

1.   Theory

The evolution of art forms across the ages has been attributed to just about everything from gigantic political and social upheavals to a lonely artist's yearning to be different. But whatever the origins, every innovation has sought to justify itself as a triumph of truth over convention.

Especially on the stage, truth-mongering has proved to be an admirably effective means of imposing novelty. In fact, the boards of Paris have probably seen no more crimes committed in the name of liberty than travesties in the name of truth. In the seventeenth century a few doctrinaires, finding contemporary stage conventions unpalatable, were able to convince both dramatist and public that a strict adherence to Aristotelian unities enhanced a play's verisimilitude. Romantics, with a relish for the grotesque and fulsome, claimed that they were merely restoring the totality of life to a falsely emasculated classical stage. And realists, quickly dubbed naturalists, began some eighty years ago to serve up slices of life trimmed of every remaining stage convention, honest peep-shows into the outside world through the fourth wall of the proscenium.

But naturalism, like every ism before it, could not long maintain its probing and critical qualities, and

soon sclerosed around certain conventions. Succeed-
ing generations of playwrights, to embody their truths,
had to devise new formulas and to overcome the handi-
cap of fighting a lie called naturalism or realism. Many
had so absorbed the precepts of naturalism that they
went on to justify their own innovations under the
old banner. Such was Maeterlinck, who for several
years saw truth in slices of silence and shreds of dreams,
and who attempted to portray this tenuous core of
human existence in his static dramas. Such was
Maeterlinck's artistic heir, Jean-Jacques Bernard,
whose "theatre of the unexpressed" more wisely
limited the silences to a play's moments of heightened
emotion. Such were the expressionists, who deliberately distorted life and depersonalized character in order
to express their own extremely personal visions of life.
And so, too, were the surrealists, who claimed to bare
man's true or inner self, and the epic realists, who in a
farrago of styles strove to dramatize social reality.

During these same years, however, there arose other
schools reflecting a fundamental break with naturalism. First came an exuberant and almost stillborn
neoromanticism, personified by Edmond Rostand.
Another movement then appeared, more positive than
the romantic reaction, one which for the first time
actually challenged naturalism at its very foundations.
The question was now raised: Is it indeed successful
for stage action to imitate reality? Must not a play
always remain a show, enacted on a recognized platform before spectators without illusions? Such a view-
point was upheld by the theatricalists, a barely discernible, unvaunted school of directors and playwrights, which originated at the turn of the century in
Russia and rapidly spread across Europe.

Theatricalism seemed to rest on two premises, one æsthetic in nature, the other psychological. It implied, to begin with, that any art is more effective and honest when its medium is exposed than when it is concealed. In theory this meant that a dramatist might intensify his hold on an audience by openly exploiting a play's artificiality or staginess. The practice, however, was often disappointing. Too many dramatists were so carried away by the æsthetic that they blinded themselves to everything *but* theatricality. Almost audible was the rising intonation of "A play is a play is a play," advanced by writers foolish enough to assume that their audience's object was to play theatre and not to experience life with fresh intensity or perspective. With that same sort of æsthetic solipsism once indulged in by symbolist poets, they permitted form to intrude upon, and eventually to choke off, content itself. It is this behavior which has given rise to that "self-conscious French stage" which David Grossvogel has recently examined in depth; and it has given rise as well to the undisguised contempt many critics now show for theatricalism: for Eric Bentley it is the surrender of literate drama to the minor stage crafts of lighting, choreography, design, and acting; for John Gassner it is the blind alley of "theatre as an end in itself."[1]

Theatricalism seemed to drive, in the second place, from a universal, deeply rooted human tendency to pretend and to savor pretending in others. Sometimes referred to as histrionic sensibility, the trait suggests

1. Eric Bentley, *The Playwright as Thinker* (New York, 1946), Chap. 10; John Gassner, *Form and Idea in Modern Theatre* (New York, Dryden Press, 1956), p. 149.

a human capacity to transform life itself into a continuous performance. This tendency led to the theatricalist actor's abandonment of character portrayal for the sake of visible performing; it led to his bolting from the make-believe of the stage environment onto the open platform. Actually, such a style of acting was far from new. On the contrary, theatricalism itself, as Gassner has observed, was not a modern phenomenon; it was simply rediscovered "after having been in vogue for some twenty-five centuries before Ibsen."[2]

The father of the modern rediscovery in France was Jacques Copeau. From the bare stage of the Vieux-Colombier, he set out to "retheatricalize theatre"—and to prepare the way for Jean Anouilh. Copeau's disciples, Louis Jouvet and Charles Dullin, together with the Pitoëffs, went on to transform and dominate the whole fabric of the French theatre world for well over a generation, popularizing such starkly theatricalist playwrights as Giraudoux, Crommelynck, and Pirandello, the works of whom were to make a vital and indelible impression on young Anouilh.

In fact, the directors of this same school were soon running up against Anouilh's own works. Anouilh himself was just twenty-one (and already turning out comedies) when he went to Jouvet: the celebrated actor-director engaged him as private secretary, and ruthlessly belittled that secretary's literary pretensions. A few years later, Anouilh approached the Pitoëffs and had more success: they were responsible for his first two hits, *Le Voyageur sans bagage* and *La Sauvage*. In 1938 Anouilh met André Barsacq, disciple of Charles Dullin and heir to his playhouse. Their as-

2. *Form and Idea*, p. 154.

sociation was long, intimate, and mutually beneficial: by 1951 Barsacq had staged ten of Anouilh's plays.

To be sure, mere associations mean no more on the stage than they do in any other arena, and if Anouilh is to be classified a theatricalist, it must be on the basis of his texts and nothing else. He did, however, in the course of a dozen articles and interviews, advance a theory of drama: it is simple, cohesive, and eminently theatricalist.

At a time when scholars are outpacing one another to "explain" theatre through its origins, whether of ancient rite or medieval ritual, at a time when even those supposedly frivolous men of the theatre are grimly expounding on the birth of drama, tracing it all the way back to primitive man's impersonation of beast to lure game—at this juncture Jean Anouilh contributes a delightfully impish theory of his own: the meaning of theatre lies in its nature as "play," that simple game of pretending which we all loved as children. Unfortunately, most of us have grown up to find ourselves more often spectators than participants at such games. We now require interpreters to maintain the make-believe before us and dramatists to supply the matter for our increasingly uninventive minds. And, for its own part, the game of theatre continues to press its demands upon us: we can never stop playing, never expect to behold reality incarnate and be passively amused. Rather must we remain willful accomplices to the game, accepting its rules and conventions, freely tasting of it with intellect and feeling.

Active complicity is essential to Anouilh's theatre. "I have always thought that we should make the audience and critics rehearse, too," says the Author in *La Grotte* (*LG,* p. 11). Once Anouilh went so far as to

upbraid his critics for an unwillingness to play *his*
game of theatre instead of their own old-fashioned
one. The metaphor was not fortuitous when he wrote
of himself: "On the one hand, the playwright (who
has all our sympathy) and, on the other, the majority
of the critics, did not decide to play the same game.
What can you do with your colored marbles when all
the 'nice' little classmates decide to play house? The
recess is a fizzle, naturally."[3]

In a word, then, theatre for Jean Anouilh is a *jeu;*
it is a game of pretending, a game of the intellect involving creator, interpreter, and spectator alike. Appropriately, his favorite dramatists of the past have all
possessed what he calls a "marvelous sense of play"—
Racine, who played with passions; Molière, who
played with human foibles; Marivaux, who played
with amorists; and last, Giraudoux, whom he regards
as the "prince of play." Interpreters are similarly
gauged—Copeau, Pitoëff, and, especially, Charles
Dullin: "From the peanut gallery of the Atelier
Theatre, contrasting with the icy splendors of Jouvet,
a revelation was about to fire several boys of my generation: theatre . . . was a warm shanty where you came
to play at make-believe, the way you did when you
were little."[4]

Pretending is probably as generic to Anouilh the
man as to Anouilh the dramatist. Take the word
minimistafia as it recurs throughout his work. In
Roméo et Jeannette the heroine, reminiscing about
her past, mentions a childhood charm, some red paper
called minimistafia, which she used to eat to find courage. Fourteen years later, in *L'Hurluberlu*, Anouilh

3. *Le Figaro* (Jan. 23, 1952).
4. Ibid. (Dec. 12, 1959).

returned to the same charm but dramatized its powers.
The General's son, Toto, admits he is afraid of another boy, and the General gives him some red blotting
paper called minimistafia: "When you feel you're going to be afraid, you bite off a little bit." And not only
does Toto immediately bite into some before a re-
proving curate, but later in the play it is the General
himself, his noble world having crumbled about him,
who asks Toto for a speck. Very solemnly, father and
son chew the red paper, seeking in it the courage to
continue playing that comedy called life. In a third
encounter:

> We were at Erquy . . . we were in the garden play-
> ing cowboys and Indians. He was General Butter-
> fly and I was private Squint-Eye—he had come
> up with that one. "Private Squint-Eye," he said,
> "go to the end of the path and see if there are any
> Indians around." I started, nearly dead with
> fright, wondering, "How can I protect papa?" He
> said, "You mustn't be afraid. Here, wait a min-
> ute." Taking on a mysterious air, he produced a
> piece of a red blotter and explained: "It's mini-
> mistafia. I have some more. Whenever you're
> afraid, you bite off a little bit and chew. See? It's
> a charm that destroys fear!"

With these words a young French actress has looked
back upon her childhood with her father, Jean
Anouilh.[5]

Accepting Anouilh's definition of theatre as a game
of the intellect, one wonders what bearing it will have
on the plays themselves. The author has explained

5. Voldemar Lestienne, "La Grande Fille de Monsieur Anouilh"
[Catherine Anouilh], *Elle* (Nov. 6, 1959), p. 58.

what it meant to him when he first embraced the notion in 1936 during the composition of *Le Voyageur sans bagage*. He no longer felt compelled to "submit" to a subject—that is, to treat it in its simple or rigorous naturalness. He discovered that an artist could and should "toy" with his material, be it in comedy or tragedy. The discovery here was simply the value of distortion—a value never too hard to defend: "A drama that has this toying resembles a musical composition. The toying won't make the drama less true, it won't even reduce its verisimilitude. On the contrary, the drama seems to draw even closer to truth as the author toys more and better with it."[6] Thus spoke Anouilh in an interview in 1936. Fifteen years later, in *La Répétition,* he was still asserting that "theatre's truth is the least natural thing in the world," and defining the playwright's task "to create—by every artifice possible—something truer than truth" (*PB,* p. 387). In illustration of these little paradoxes, he has on various occasions recounted the following anecdote: "A child, when he wants to persuade his mother not to send him to school, will pretend to be ill. Generally, he is a poor actor; his mother knows he's not really sick. But when this same child plays at being ill in front of other children, he reveals himself to be a remarkable actor. This, essentially, is the truth of the theatre."[7]

Pausing before so much truth, we recall that Picasso once dispatched the same notion in his aphorism, "Art is a lie that shows us the truth." The stage, of course, is just a *bigger* lie—so big, say a few writers, that the

6. *Les Nouvelles littéraires* (Jan. 10, 1946).
7. Ibid. (March 27, 1937).

only truth it can possibly show us is itself: "In the theatre *acting* is the essential truth, a truth more important than the psychological background of events," wrote Giraudoux in his first play.[8] Fortunately, Jean Anouilh escaped the pit of preciosity; he has employed the lie of the stage to convey important truths, truths about life and people.

For the moment we shall not dwell on the exact nature of these truths, but instead turn to the deformations that enclose them. Significantly, Anouilh has not set them in just any lies. Rather, he has framed his psychological and metaphysical truths in the most glaring, hackneyed, and threadbare conventions of the stage. Convinced that theatre is play, he has not shrunk from the consequence that the more obvious, the more accomplished the playing (and the French word for playing, *le jeu,* also means acting), the better the theatre. It follows that moments of supreme truth in these works occur amidst the greatest pretending: it is during a rehearsal (*La Répétition*) of a scene from Marivaux that an aging aristocrat encounters love for the first time in his life; for over an hour the petals of a daisy (*La Marguerite*) are stripped away, revealing love's many facets, but the horrid and naked truth of this passion does not emerge until the final curtain falls on two children playing house.

Theatre for Jean Anouilh means the opening of a big red curtain; and when the curtain has opened, the faces of theatricalism will be varied. Over the years they have included the use of a chorus (*Antigone*), spectacle (*Le Bal des voleurs*), distorted time sequences (*L'Alouette*), distorted history (anachronisms, the

8. *Siegfried,* III.2.

Saxon Becket), visible fantasy (the make-believe horse-back riding in *L'Alouette*), wildly incredible stock situations (identical twins, long-lost sons), the play within the play (whereby the artificiality of the secondary play is legitimized), or even arch reminders to the audience that they are witnessing a show. But these are only the trappings of Anouilh's theatricalism. There is far more behind them.

2. Form

How will a theatricalist playwright approach form? It goes without saying that he will cast his work in some highly stylized and artificial mold. Theoretically, this mold can be *any* of the stage's traditional forms—ancient tragedy, vaudeville, morality, no matter—so long as it is easily recognizable and, presumably, is treated with a boldness, detachment, and irreverence bordering on parody. So runs the theory. But like most artists worth generalizing about, Jean Anouilh has proceeded less from theory than from taste. Although his handling of form may occasionally have been theatricalist (at least since he adopted the æsthetic of the *jeu*), the structure of his plays cannot be explained entirely by any theory.

By the time Anouilh came to Paris from Bordeaux in 1928, theatricalism was already a rising, if not a reigning, force on the capital's stages. True, the aspiring playwright was not yet twenty, but he already owed the naturalist past a legacy large enough to influence his first endeavors. And so, despite the early revelations of Giraudoux and Pirandello, he set about writing well-made plays cut to the timeworn patterns of Scribe and Sardou. *L'Hermine* and *Jézabel,* the earliest "pièces noires," were both tightly constructed murder stories. Our interest is held in the former by a series of melodramatic questions: Will Frantz really murder Monime's aunt? Will Monime let him? Will the police trip up Frantz? Will Monime sully the ermine's spotless white coat and cause him to surrender? In *Jézabel* suspense is constantly maintained by withholding bits of information: Just why has Marc fled Jacqueline? What is this report he is awaiting and upon which his future actions depend? What are his relations with the maid? And so on. Certainly nowhere has Anouilh obeyed the laws of lesser stagecraft and practiced the art of preparation as conscientiously as in these early pieces.

Within a few years, however, the dramatist was able to shake off this residual naturalism. He simply turned from plotting to playing; he stopped *toiling* with stories and began *toying* with them instead. There was something disturbingly cavalier about this new approach to dramatic form, and perhaps, in consequence, Anouilh was given to overenthusiasm in the defense of his views:

> I know that a certain school of playwrights, highly esteemed by their masters, keeps on constructing "well-made" plays and mincing plots, convinced, even now, that salvation lies in this direction, despite the drubbing by Pirandello's *Six Characters* and the breath of liberty and poetry brought by Giraudoux.[1]

> I have put in, personally, about twenty years, and some of my colleagues, masters or workmates, from Giraudoux to Achard or Salacrou . . . since the First World War have been fighting to strangle plots, to kill—to the point of reducing to a mum-

1. *Le Figaro* (Jan. 23, 1952).

my—the notion of the "well-made play" that has reigned in French Theatre since Scribe. Pirandello, in a stroke of genius, the importance of which can never be exaggerated, took the trouble one day of completely asphyxiating the notion with his *Six Characters in Search of an Author*. Well, in spite of this execution . . .[2]

In their blanket rejection of formal plot, these words may recall other voices from the French past: Vigny as he defended *Chatterton* or even Racine before *Bérénice*. But when we turn to Anouilh's plays themselves, we realize that it is not plots per se he would execute, but rather the primacy of plot, that primacy which under Scribe and Sardou led to the atrophy of every other legitimate value in drama.

As a matter of fact, just a cursory glance at *Six Characters in Search of an Author* confirms that, all the oratory to the contrary, this play did not strangle even its own plot. Granted, the work's principal merit lies well beyond the story line in its fantastic and ingenious premise. Still, as the initial shock subsides, our curiosity focuses on the drama of these six beings. Grounded in adultery, that staple of nineteenth-century theatre, this drama slowly unfolds before us, bit by suspenseful bit. The first act suggests a crucial scene, one upon which the entire play rests. In the second act this sensational scene is finally enacted as the father engages his own stepdaughter at a brothel. And from here on, interest wanes as the third act degenerates into fitful acrobatics on reality and nonreality, acting and nonacting, permanence and mobility.

Fascinating parallels to Pirandello's play appear in

2. *Opéra* (March 7, 1951).

Anouilh's *La Grotte*. The dramatist presents *La Grotte* (sincerely so, we are informed) as a play he was unable to write, and not as a parody of Pirandello, Ghelderode, et al. After the actor who portrays Anouilh has offered the public a few alternative opening scenes, the central device takes over. Once again it is that of characters who assume life and impose their story, no longer on a group of actors but on their own creator, who demurs before his offsprings' bleak destinies. The actual plot has thickened since Pirandello's time, adultery becoming now simply another figure on a broad mosaic of murder, rape, abortion, white slavery, and class warfare. Ironically, it is only by coincidence that the murderer is discovered and the plot resolved just as the final curtain descends; for the vital point here is that it was precisely because Anouilh insisted on subordinating plot to the impact of theme and characters that he was unable to write the play in the first place. Galsworthy once said that "character is situation," meaning that characters can fully reveal themselves only in context. The brutal situations of *La Grotte* have obviously been invented and arranged to give meaning and emotional wings to the characters, not to tell a story.

On several occasions Anouilh has behaved just as one might expect a theatricalist to behave: he has openly parodied the workings of some conventional genre. Early in *L'Invitation au château,* for example, the protagonist sets the scene: "I love no one, young lady. That's what is going to allow me to organize with complete serenity of mind this evening's little comedy. For I am determined that tonight it will be I who organizes the comedy. . . . I've constructed an entire scenario" (*PB,* pp. 40, 43). And from this point we are off on a spree of mistaken identities, peripeteia, and wildly complicated intrigue. Nothing is believable in this stylized piece built on the tired old prop of identical twins. The spectators may just as well be at a Feydeau play, wondering how in the world the author will extricate himself from what seems to be an impossible situation or bring a combustible pair of characters face to face. For our attention is ever drawn to the author, to the showman whose genius has begotten this web of fantasy and whose wind will eventually blow it all away. Someone once said that plots are like jigsaw puzzles, amusing for the man putting them together but dull for anyone watching. Anouilh, in plays like *L'Invitation, Le Bal des voleurs,* or *Cécile,* shows how amusing they can be for us all, if only they are handled with theatricalist irony, and if only they are not taken too seriously.

Just as Anouilh recklessly overcolored some plots, he has reduced others to flat banality. *Colombe* is nothing but the account of a soldier returning home to a faithless wife, *L'Hurluberlu* that of an aging husband's attempts to discover who has been flirting with his young wife. A few plays actually have had no story at all. Next to nothing happens in either *L'Orchestre* or *Ornifle* until the closing instants: in the one a melodramatic cellist retires to the ladies' room and shoots herself; in the other an aging Don Juan, en route to a rendezvous, drops dead off-stage to a choir accompaniment of "Jesus, Thou Art Hiding."

Complicated or plain, many plots are openly derivative. Scholars have already identified a number of possible sources. *Le Voyageur sans bagage* points to Giraudoux's *Siegfried; Léocadia* to Sarment's *Léopold le bien-aimé; Cécile* to Marivaux's *Ecole des mères*—to name but a few. Not only plots but occasional discourse is borrowed. *Antigone* has its passages from Sophocles, *L'Alouette* its exchanges from Jeanne d'Arc's authentic trial, and *La Petite Molière* several scenes lifted wholly from *L'Amour médecin*.[3] Asked to comment on this latter appropriation, Anouilh replied to an interviewer: "All works of literature . . . are basically plagiarisms except the first, which is unknown."[4] Ironically, he stole the epigram itself: "Plagiarism is at the basis of all works of literature except the first, which is unknown," had said Giraudoux a generation earlier (*Siegfried,* I.6).

Within these unoriginal plots, many of the devices are stale and freely repeated from play to play: husbands are burdened by invalid wives; poor orphans are bullied into *mariages de convenance* and thence to adultery; respectable fathers keep colliding with their illegitimate sons; unexplained messages call people away; the traveler without luggage bears an identifying scar—not on his ankles, in the tragic way, nor even on his bottom, in comic fashion, but on his shoulder, after the melodramatic school. And in case all these hackneyed plots and devices should fail to light our path, there are the program synopses which at an Anouilh production never bother to hide the endings. Thus, even before the curtain rises, we know that Thomas à Becket will betray his friend Henry II when the latter names him archbishop; we know that the scatterbrained General will have as much success

---

3. See Anouilh, *Antigone,* ed. David I. Grossvogel (Cambridge, Mass., 1958); Jack Brooking, "Jeanne d'Arc, the Trial Notes, and Anouilh," *Theatre Annual* (1959).

4. *Paris-Match* (June 13, 1959), p. 98.

conspiring as Don Quixote had jousting with wind-mills, and that at the close of the play his fellow conspirators will have deserted him, his wife will be about to do so, and he will take it all stoically, remaining "inconsolable but gay." This trick of dispelling our interest in plot is analogous to various procedures in the realm of painting: by distorting, obfuscating, and even discarding a canvas' logical center of interest, such as a woman's face or a ballerina's torso, the painter, too, hopes to draw the observer's attention away from the formal story back toward the work of art itself, to its composition, and thence to its inner truth. The conclusion to be drawn from Jean Anouilh's conventional and shallow plotting, then, is not that the writer is uninventive; it is that he regards plots as valueless save for their theatricality.

"The last act of a play is its own judgment of itself," wrote playwright-critic Gabriel Marcel, and there is much truth in his observation. Racine's endings are absolute and inevitable, and are said to reflect the imperiousness of his terribly ordered universe. Molière's endings, although now recognized to be more logical and dramatically sound than was once assumed,[5] are still overtly contrived; if the spectator is perceptive, he can see the essential evils still before him, unchanged. And Anouilh's denoucments, especially since 1936, bear out Marcel's notion. Indeed, it is not by chance that Marcel (who is one of France's most sensitive critics of Anouilh) wrote these words while reviewing *Le Voyageur sans bagage,* Anouilh's first consciously theatricalist work.

5. See J. D. Hubert, *Molière and the Comedy of Intellect* (Berkeley, Cal., 1962).

The story concerns the good-hearted Gaston, an amnesic war veteran claimed by several families. Confronted by what proves to be his real family, Gaston balks at the burden of a sinful past; he denies his identity. Suddenly, as if by magic, there appears another family in the person of a young orphan remotely related to a missing soldier. Gaston accepts an inauthentic identity and remains pure. "Never have I seen more clearly to what extent an artificial denouement retrospectively colors an entire play," said Marcel.[6] And it is so: the ending comes as a shock to most spectators who, until this moment, have not realized that Anouilh has been playing with them all along. This is why so many people have condemned the artifice that permits an English boy to wander on stage after the actual completion of the play and offer the protagonist a rosy alternative to his black condition. It seems reasonable that, had he so wished, Anouilh could have terminated this "pièce noire" on a truly black note, with Gaston shouldering his guilt-edged identity or retreating into a selfless asylum existence. He might just as easily have finished the play in pink and made the ending more plausible. But he did not. Instead, he chose to emphasize by every means the artificiality of his ending, implying thereby that only on the stage can man so easily escape his guilt: gay music springs up for the first time in the play to accompany the boy's movements; the circumstances surrounding the boy's family are utterly preposterous; at a postwar Paris revival the role of the little boy was played by a grown woman.

A dozen years later, in *La Valse des toréadors*,

6. Gabriel Marcel, *L'Heure théâtrale* (Paris, Plon, 1959), p. 89.

Anouilh specified just what sort of denouement he prefers:

> THE GENERAL: . . . Doctor, I can feel everything going to pieces. How will this all end?
>
> THE DOCTOR: The way things do in life, or the way they used to in the theatre, back when it was still good. A tidy ending, not too sad on the surface, and which fools really no one— and a little later: curtain.   [*PG,* p. 187]

After theorizing, Anouilh went on to illustrate his thesis with this black farce's own rosy ending. Unfortunately, it was an ending which *did* fool a number of persons: it fooled everyone who took it literally enough to be offended by its patent falseness. By what it failed to say, the sketchy denouement of *La Valse* reflected the author's lofty unconcern for plot. The incident which first set the play in motion was Ghislaine de Sainte-Euverte's discovery of some compromising letters from the General's wife to her doctor. Although the authenticity of these letters is vaguely implied, we are never told how Ghislaine—who lives at the other end of France—ever came upon them in the first place. (The more pedestrian British film version showed Ghislaine purchasing the unmailed letters from one of the General's servants.)

Similar jagged ends are left in *La Répétition ou l'amour puni.* Héro does the punishing, aided and abetted by the melodramatic expedient of a false telegram. While his friend the Count is away, Héro plays: he seduces and destroys the Count's first love, Lucile. Next morning, next act, the Count returns to a shattered idyl, but he does not even seem aware of the foul play. At the other extreme, the less complicated stories have nothing even approaching a denouement. *Colombe* simply stops when the heroine has sufficiently explained to her husband why she is leaving him. *Pauvre Bitos* is over when the nasty party is over, and neither Bitos nor his antagonists have changed one jot, nothing has been resolved, nothing accomplished. Whether tidy, jagged, or missing, then, the denouements are a further indication of Anouilh's nonchalance in regard to plotting.

A distinction should be made between the denouement proper and the final trait which Anouilh so often tacks onto his plays. Sometimes a brief exchange, more often a minature tableau—these traits form an ironic commentary on what has preceded, and convey, perhaps better than the denouements, the author's judgment of his work. Typical is the close of *Médée*: after Jason has purged himself of childish ideals (and of their reductio ad absurdum, the death wish), after Médée has vilified Jason, preached intransigence, and in a moment of dramatic frenzy taken her own life— now, two servants enter the stage. In the soft light of dawn they speak of humble things, of harvest, bread, the simple tasks men must perform to live out each day. In subtle counterpoint to Médée's ravings, these words linger with us after the play has ended; they confirm our impression that at last Anouilh may have cast off his own youthful idealism. *Léocadia's* denouement is reinforced by a fanciful postscript. Prince Albert has just abandoned Léocadia's world of hyperbole and invention for Amanda's world of simplicity and truth, and the piece closes as the Prince's aunt and uncle shoot from the sky a monstrous and vulgar bird: spectators are assured that the extravagant Léocadia has likewise been effaced from Albert's memory. As for the final verdict in *Ardèle,* Anouilh's trial of love: when the story has ended two children enter the blackened stage under a pinpoint spot. Decked in their parents' clothes, they begin to play house, expressing their love for one another, as the curtain falls, in a brutal and odious struggle.

But there is more to dramatic form than plotting. Even the Scribean notion of the well-made play, attacked by Anouilh, contains other traits besides a vigorous story line. The recipe also calls for a tight structure: all the action is to be squeezed forward to the moment of crisis. Predictably, young Anouilh's first melodramas *were* tightly constructed. *Jézabel,* for example, takes place just before and after the murder of Marc's father. *L'Hermine* devotes one act to establishing motivations for a murder, one act to the murder itself, and one act to its solution.

Although Anouilh still turns out an occasional tightly wrought piece, such as *Ardèle,* he has generally developed a freer and more flexible approach. This tendency is particularly evident in the historically oriented plays where, rather than confine his action to one crucial incident, the dramatist has preferred to stretch it out over a number of episodes. Consider *Becket,* which the author claims is a tragedy of friendship: the moment he becomes Archbishop of Canterbury, Thomas à Becket abruptly switches allegiance from his friend Henry Plantagenet to the Church, Henry's traditional foe. Now Anouilh might easily have situated his play just after Becket's *volte-face,* during the first incident of disaffection between the two men, at that moment when each realized that the breach was absolute and the conflict irreconcilable. But instead of crowding his story into one moment of

dramatic intensity, he composed an historical narra-
tive whose frescoes cover almost three decades, take
place in several countries, and sweep across medieval
society from sovereign to courtesan, from peasant to
pope. Scenes of tragedy, low farce, violence, austerity,
and pure spectacle succeed one another in this pan-
oramic work, which seems consciously patterned after
Shakespeare. Diffuse as the story is, it does inevitably
contain several scenes of disaffection, and one in particular of overpowering intensity (*PC*, pp. 267–77).

Even more fragmented than *Becket* is the writer's
next play, *La Grotte*, where the numerous scenes follow no discernible pattern until the climactic last half-
hour. Yet a few of them are among the tautest and
most electrifying of Anouilh's theatre. Apparently the
playwright learned that he could generate as much
emotion in the space of a few moments as he could
in an hour of gradually mounting tension. The significant point, then, is that a loosely and whimsically
constructed play may jolt, envelop, and illumine the
spectator as deeply and as repeatedly as a more ordered,
sustained work.

A final attribute of the well-made play as perpe-
trated by Scribe and Sardou is its legendary freedom
from all extraneous material. Such a rule may smack
less of "sardoodledom," Shaw's word for the cult of
play carpentry, than of classicism, and, in effect, it is
one of the theatre's tritest dicta: every utterance and
every bit of stage business in this terribly abbreviated
art form must develop either the action, the characterization, or the central theme. Beholding Racine's
plays, for example, one has the feeling that each line
has a vital bearing on the whole, that each scene leads
one inexorably closer to the tragic outcome. In

Anouilh's works, on the other hand, we keep stumbling upon *mots d'auteur,* lines that are plainly unrelated to the body of the work and whose only justification is that they must have tickled the author's fancy. Plots are interrupted, dropped, and resumed with graceful abandon. It was not until 1959, in his program notes to *Becket,* that Anouilh admitted a proclivity to inserting facile vaudeville jokes in his plays, but he had been doing so for well over twenty years. Sometimes there were digressive anecdotes, sometimes easy historical or nationalistic mots, like Becket's "Honor for an Englishman . . . has always meant 'success'" (*PC,* p. 194), or Mme. Alexandra's circa 1890 assertion, "Do you believe in the Métro? It's a chimera" (*PB,* p. 228). The origin of these and other liberties must no doubt be placed in Anouilh's all-important 1936 decision to toy with his subject matter rather than to submit to it. Accordingly, the first "playful" effort, *Le Voyageur sans bagage,* although it is a relatively short piece and has been staged without intermission, is nevertheless a loosely constructed one. It opens with the duchess Dupont-Dufort unleashing a string of jokes and puns, many of which have no bearing whatsoever on the events to follow, and whose expository value is at best incidental. The play is warm with humanity; its theme is provocative; and one wonders whether it would not have benefited from a less fanciful exposition.

More typical are the liberties of composition in the recent plays. *L'Hurluberlu* is the story of a misanthropic reformer (like all reformers, he is a misanthrope to the extent that he mistakes humanity for inhumanity) who would save his country but who cannot even govern his own household. In performance the comedy seems marvelously well constructed: all the little episodes cohere about the hero's ineffectualness. But the fact is that the first two acts are composed largely of hors d'oeuvres, in the etymological sense, and it is the hors d'oeuvres—anecdotes and parodies—which invariably produce the biggest laughs. Conceivably, *Zim! boum!,* the recited parody of the avant-garde theatre, supports the reactionary hero's contention that France today is wallowing in decay; but it is preceded by another parody, of the old-fashioned *théâtre de patronage,* which certainly does not. What is more, as the spectator's thoughts naturally drift back to a more famous misanthrope (even the titles encourage the rapport: *L'Hurluberlu ou le réactionnaire amoureux* and *Le Misanthrope ou l'atrabilaire amoureux*), he realizes that Molière's parodies were much better integrated into his plays: Alceste was reacting to a society where just this sort of precious reading was rampant and where it habitually drew exaggerated praise. No such readings mark our own decadent era, where theatre itself plays but a minor part.

If Anouilh's plays are not well-made, they do have a certain structure or, more accurately, a movement to them. This movement is over and above ordinary stage rhythm—that flux of gravity and gaiety, of assault and diversion, of talk and action, which any competent dramatist must establish to hold onto his audience. (Anouilh once defined playwriting skill as the "ability to land on all fours," meaning the ability to maintain constant control over one's audience.) As may be expected, Anouilh handles rhythm effortlessly, so effortlessly that in some of his plays (*L'Hurluberlu* or *Becket,* for example) moments of tension and release succeed one another with truly predictable regularity. The characteristic pattern of Anouilh's theatre is of a different sort. There is a clear tendency to begin each piece in lightness and joy, to progress through a number of climaxes toward pessimism and truth, then to veer about abruptly and end in make-believe. This movement of penetration, this shifting of tonality or mood, is the only structure we find in his theatre. It is also a very logical one: if there is something funny about a person—for instance, the way he opens beer cans with his nose—it is going to make us laugh right now, while we are still surprised, and not in an hour when we have grown accustomed to him. And then, who can say? Maybe in an hour, after we have got to know the poor fellow, we'll be more inclined to cry or to drink with him than to laugh at him. Novelty, exposure, alienation, identification—these are the elementary and banal laws of comedy that Anouilh naturally obeys as he makes his characters ludicrous on first appearance and profound or pathetic only when the audience has got to know them. Indeed, he has been so adept at this practice that he has been accused of sadism: he creates phantoms of pastel gaiety merely to impale them, several acts later, through their black souls.

La Valse des toréadors offers the clearest illustration of this movement. The farce opens on a series of grossly comic frames: the General is reproached by his wife for his "pangenital" curiosity, he flippantly dismisses her and his ungainly daughters as a trio of monsters, and he dictates some racy memoirs to a startled and chaste secretary. Enters Ghislaine de Sainte-Euverte, for seventeen years the General's near-mistress. She simpers and swoons and roundly declares she will soon be rid of the General's wife and her own maidenhood to boot. Once the *gaulois* tone has been established, the doctor enters the scene. He and the General set to talking, and it is deep, grown-up talk, theirs, all about fear, the soul, and life itself. In the fourth act the General again confronts his wife, only this time in deadly earnest, and after some hideous exchanges he nearly strangles her. The fifth act is a return to pinkness, and amidst the most threadbare contrivances, the curtain falls.

If *La Valse* is open to criticism, it is not for the multiplicity of tones, and certainly not for their gradual darkening, but for the clumsiness with which the General's and the doctor's speculations are attached to the rest of the work: the two men ramble over incidents artificially extracted from their remote and private pasts. If only their discourse had risen more naturally and more directly from the dramatized actions, Anouilh might well have come close to writing that ideal play which Shaw once defined as progressing from exposition to action and culminating in discussion.

Actually, it was on a number of other counts that Parisian critics attacked *La Valse des toréadors*. Their principal charge was that the play lacked a point of view, that it had no direction, no unity: it was just a chaos of vaudeville, tragedy, high comedy, melodrama, and farce. In a sense, the critics were right: the play does lack unity, and what—so runs the cliché—is a work of art without unity? Plenty, we should say, when that work is a drama. For better or for worse, the key words in theatre are not merely unity, coherence, and validity. They can also be intensity, impact, and illusion. A play survives not only because spectators admire, in retrospect, its balance of structure or its coherency of point of view, but also because during a performance it overpowers them, blinds them, and thrusts at them a vision of life more intense and penetrating than that to which they are accustomed.[7] In a stimulating essay entitled "The Fallacy of Unity," John Gassner has pointed out that what spectators absorb in the theatre is a "series of related flashes rather than a steady illumination." Too many critics, he adds,

> forget the importance of the moment-by-moment effect in the audience. They overlook the fact that a play is an unfolding experience, that drama is a process interesting precisely as a process to the spectator, since he views the events only as they succeed each other on the stage. They think only of the final result, forgetting that for the audience each scene and subscene, each encounter between characters and revelation is also a *result,* or, temporarily, an end in itself.[8]

Theatre's *summum bonum,* then, lies not in form but in isolated flashes of dramatic intensity. Stendhal said the same thing over a hundred years ago. And so, more recently, has Jean Anouilh: "Leave the laws of architecture to construction experts. Theatre is a game of the intellect, and the intellect, like the bee, can very well make its honey by jumping from detail to detail."[9]

7. Even the epic theatre alienates the viewer's emotions in order to involve more deeply his social conscience. See Wayne C. Booth, *The Rhetoric of Fiction* (Chicago, 1961), pp. 122 ff., for a discussion of psychic distance.

8. John Gassner, *The Theatre in Our Times* (New York, Crown, 1960) pp. 462, 458.

9. *Opéra* (March 7, 1951).

3. Caricature

Once upon a time Brunetière was able to discuss characterization and plotting with inconsiderate simplicity. A playwright, he said, could subordinate character to plot, as Corneille had done, by first discovering a plot and then setting up agents within it. Or else he could subordinate plot to character, as Racine had done, by first establishing a character and then finding the situation that would best reveal him. The only difference, he felt, is that the characters of Racine necessarily seem more alive to us than the agents of Corneille.

If the world has grown more complex since Brunetière's days, so have the characters in it. Not a few observers are convinced that, thanks to Pirandello, theatre has once and for all been purged of plots and their lifeless agents. Yet today's stage fauna often seem less alive or developed than those of the past. Jean Anouilh's characters, in particular, lack that comforting substance many of us seek in the theatre. This is all the more disturbing because, as a number of critics would have it, Anouilh practices the Racinean formula stated above, writing his plays around specific characters. In point of fact, nobody really knows how Anouilh composes his dramas. (We are personally more inclined to accept the guess of his longtime as-

sociate, actor Christian Lude, that settling upon a
theme tends to be Anouilh's point of departure.) But
regardless of his method of writing, regardless of the
force with which the creatures have lived and asserted
themselves in his mind, one thing is certain: by the
time they reach the stage, they are closer to caricatures
than to real people. And it is not simply because
Anouilh is a theatricalist that this is so. Pirandello,
Thornton Wilder, Salacrou—to name but a few prac-
titioners of the same æsthetic—sometimes found it
more effective to unleash quite realistic people within
their play worlds. Even Giraudoux, despite an occasional pasteboard prop for poetic or intellectual display, created stage people that seem more human than
many of Anouilh's caricatures. The latter's rationale,
then, would seem to be a personal and arbitrary one.

Why caricatures in the first place, one wonders. In
an interview in 1951, after once again stressing that
he had always considered theatre a game of the intellect, Anouilh said quite simply, "Isn't caricaturing
the most important game of the intellect?"[1] An un-
conventional theory, to say the least. But though it
would be a tough case to argue before a dean, before
the footlights Anouilh's remark does have a certain
validity. The dictionary defines a caricature as a picture or description "ludicrously exaggerating the peculiarities or defects of persons or things." Then every
stage character, we should say, tends somewhat toward
caricature: as there is rarely enough time during a
play to present a whole personality, whatever we may
think we mean by "whole personality," dramatists
must settle on presenting only those facets of a man

1. *Arts* (Nov. 16, 1951).

vital to the situation at hand, and may even exaggerate
these for the sake of clarity. Furthermore, they must
concentrate their effects: too thorough a portrayal of
the minor characters risks dispersing our attention
and diverting us from the essential business. And so,
no matter how real the creatures of a playwright's
fancy may have been when he conceived them, they
must inevitably be abbreviated, deformed, and somewhat devitalized by the exigencies of the medium, to
finish as derisory stage people. Much of the life-giving
epiphenomena will have been hacked away as the
author sees his characters' stage life hanging by the
tenuous threads of a few scored traits and, even more
perilously, by the possibly bungling misinterpretations of the actors. Nevertheless, it is precisely the actor
who more than compensates for the artificiality of the
average stage character; for no matter how contrived
or conventional a personage may be, the actor willy-
nilly thrusts life upon him as he embodies the role.
We can see now how relatively unimportant it is for
a playwright to be able to create living three-dimensional characters—obviously much less so than for the
novelist, whose skill, until the recent proliferation of
antinovels, was often gauged on just this score.

Nor should it surprise us that one of Anouilh's most
successful works, *Ardèle,* is peopled exclusively by
caricatures. Actually, these marionettes or puppets,
as they are often called, are only relatively more contrived than the conventional stage figure. Rather than
compose his character about a number of significant
traits, Anouilh simply pounces on one or two trivial
traits, draws them out, and parades a disfigured and
often ridiculous creature before the public. His dis-

tinctiveness lies in his intention: he deliberately flat-
tens characters into caricatures. He once went on rec-
ord to explain exactly why. The occasion was the January 1952 opening of *La Valse des toréadors,* a play, as
we have seen, censured for its lack of unity. But also
attacked were the poor acting, the miscasting that
threw youthful Claude Sainval into the role of the retired, burned-out General, and the failure of any of
its characters to come alive. Faced with such hostility,
the author held his peace for a fortnight; then in *Le
Figaro* of January 23 he riposted with vehemence. The
text deserves to be quoted at length, for it is the virtual
ars poetica of Jean Anouilh:

> Now there's a great play! There at last is a
> playwright who understands that theatre is above
> all a free game of the intellect, that verisimilitude,
> a carefully directed plot, skillfully regulated en-
> trances and exits, are nothing.
>
> Indeed, nothing is believable in this story of
> General Saint-Pé, who waited seventeen years for
> Mlle. de Sainte-Euverte, the woman he loved, only
> to lose her in ten minutes; and yet, everything is
> true. Devices of caricature and vaudeville—
> which must be compared to the voluntary de-
> formations practiced by a school of modern paint-
> ing—marvelously introduce us, thanks to the
> dancelike staging of Roland Piétri and the sets
> of Jean-Denis Malclès, into the droll and dis-
> quieting world of bad dreams. Here is a scenario
> by Mack Sennett or Feydeau, beneath whose plot
> lie *real* emotions, sometimes tragic ones, but
> which are rendered inoffensive and proper to the

game of the intellect by the deformations of caricature. It's up to us to play with them! The game
and the colors are without danger, the spirit
fundamentally sound, the conclusion eminently
moral (the general is harshly punished for having
been cowardly before life and love), and we laugh
from one end to the other, even (and especially)
when we ought to be crying.

Still, this is good comedy, and well played.
Claude Sainval has succeeded in the feat of being
both a marionette, as the author asked him to
be, and a human character. How many great actors in Paris, nourished in the grand tradition,
can still be marionettes, and not limit a character to themselves and to the mannerisms that
have made them loved? How many are able to
be only a pretext of flesh and bones, about which
each spectator can reconstruct the imaginary person of his dreams? Marvelous General Saint-Pé,
so unreal that no shopgirl will ever dream of
going to the stage door for his autograph. There
at last is a poetic actor!

We see two central ideas here, and they are applicable not only to *La Valse des toréadors* but to all of
Anouilh's theatre since the early "pièces noires": first,
that the artist employs a caricatural deformation to
mask and soften his vitriolic truths, and, secondly,
that he depersonalizes these caricatures into empty
frames for each spectator to fill and experience sub-
jectively. Expressionism, too, was built about such
techniques of distortion and depersonalization. But
whereas the expressionist playwright was didactic, and
distorted characters in order to accentuate his message,

Anouilh the showman, sensing his truth too black to be countenanced directly by an audience, Anouilh the *sauvage*, loath to bore, or preach at, his public, deforms his characters in order to attenuate the truth by making it diverting. We can grasp his position at once from a single line: toward the close of *Ardèle* the Count says, "Fortunately we're ridiculous, otherwise this story would be really too sad" (*PG*, p. 65).

In recent years the author has explained his caricatures in a slightly different way. "I'm through with tragedy! At last I understand. Of course everything is ugly. Of course everything is sad. So what? Everyone knows it. The soul must be purged. By laughter. The only virile attitude before the human condition is comedy." Assuredly, these are Anouilh's own thoughts, though they are here attributed to his adopted and adapted forefather, Molière (*MO*, p. 25). Musset was once moved by the deep sadness of Molière's virile gaiety; Anouilh now finds in Molière, within the mold of comedy, "the blackest theatre in the literature of all time."[2] And Anouilh implies that by casting his own black theatre in a similar mold—the pink mold of comedy, caricatures, and conventions—he was being equally virile and wise. For a dozen years, in plays and miscellanea, he has virtually been saying as much: "At the final reckoning . . . we shall realize that only those who have made us laugh have done us a really good turn on this earth. . . . They alone made us forget death"; "Those who have entertained others will be to the right of God. You cheat death by preventing people from thinking of themselves"; "To make men

2. Anouilh, "Présence de Molière," M. Renaud and J.-L. Barrault, *Cahiers*, 26 (Paris, Julliard, 1959). 5.

forget for three hours their condition and death is a good trade, and a useful one."[3]

Just what are these caricatures made of, and how are they put together? The type we encounter most often is the individual out of touch with reality—with his own reality. Rampant are the fools who picture themselves with Gallic grandeur. Isabelle's mother lumbers onto the set of *L'Invitation au château* crying, "What luxury! What refinement! What sumptuousness! Here is an atmosphere, child, where I can become my true self again" (*PB,* p. 21). Technically, the spectators do not yet have any proof that she is talking nonsense, but as the play continues, the fact is confirmed: she sees herself as a Great Artist, and swept away by the imputed romance of her situation, she is soon gushing alexandrines. At the other extreme we see figures equally burlesque, equally out of touch with reality, but who debase existence, who measure the world from the mean vantage point of their own egotism, and who embrace all values now with their outstretched palms (as do the guards in *Pauvre Bitos,* assessing the Reign of Terror in terms of personal monetary gain), now with their bowels (a feat Mme. Georges brings off in *Colombe*).

A number of the caricatures fall into easy stereotypes. That last vestige of dignity in our crass world, the butler, whose very speech and manner approach parody, seems especially to have appealed to Anouilh. There have been, too, the obvious national stereotypes: the Italians with their *combinazione,* or the Englishmen with their sportsmanship, effeteness, cult of the gentleman, and commercial ethos.

3. *PG,* p. 241; *Paris-Match* (June 13, 1959), p. 95; *Opéra* (March 7, 1951).

Another common device for mounting caricatures is the use of multiples: two men, identically rigged, suddenly swoop onto the stage, and, as Bergson said we must, we see them as a dehumanized, ludicrous pair. It is a sure thing, and well Anouilh must have known it, for he has used the devise repeatedly. Take, for instance, the entrance of those pitiful puppets of *Colombe,* Poète-Chéri and Desfournettes, designated simply by "two big collars, two duck-tail haircuts, two pairs of mustaches, two top hats, two frock coats, two canes" (*PB,* p. 197); or the confrontation in *Léocadia* of the two maître d'hôtels, who not only look like brothers but talk like the same man (we recall the author's excellent reading of his own play, broadcast in France); or the General's daughters in *La Valse des toréadors:* "Estelle and Sidonie enter, big gawks of about twenty, still children; ringlets, elf locks and ear coils, ridiculous little-girls' frocks" (*PG,* p. 95). Why two? Not merely because two monsters are more awful than one, but because we take multiples less seriously, because in this last play the two girls will experience the same passion for the same lad, be collectively spurned, and attempt a "bisuicide."

There is no point in presenting a catalogue of caricatures, for it must be clear by now that Anouilh has merely followed the traditional recipes of farce. Significantly, he hasn't flinched before even the crudest devices. In *Episode de la vie d'un auteur* everyone is made to wear a false nose. In his adaptation of *The Importance of Being Earnest,* Anouilh kept remarkably close to the original text, but jovially turned a tea-time tiff into a washerwoman's brawl. And not only is there an occasional punch, pinch, scream, or chase in his works, there may also be downright clowning

by the actors. Directing *Ornifle,* for example, Anouilh
had character actor Louis de Funès (known in this
country through films) play the role of Machetu with
his full bag of tricks: grunts, shrugs, twitches, eye-rolls,
"r"-rolls, etc. And Machetu, of course, like Ledadu,
Bitos, Robinet, or Galopin, is just another of those
ridiculous-sounding farcical names the author gives
his children. The word is really bland when we compare it to the more gaulois names sometimes heard in
the plays: Culogratti, Lepet, Foutriquet, Chancrad,
and so forth. Inevitably, some of these traditional devices are more successful than others. The least felicitous in today's light are the repetitive tricks of the
early pieces: Marie-Anne of *L'Hermine* is so completely circumscribed by her spinster's anxiety that her
lines, intended to be cumulatively funny, are instead
cumulatively maddening. Similarly, the caricatures
built around verbal tics or parrotism miscarry today.

In Jean Anouilh's handling of character, a distinct
evolution has occurred. Through the years more and
more of his people have found themselves reduced to
caricatures; at the same time they have grown less and
less consistent.

Actually, even in his earliest efforts Anouilh was
creating puppets. It is likely he was born with the
caricaturist's acute sense of the comic in people. Had
Daumier left but a few words behind, they might well
have resembled these by Anouilh: "We can wound one
another, betray one another, massacre one another
under more or less noble pretexts, inflate ourselves
with false grandeur: *we are funny.* Nothing else, every
single one of us, including those whom we call our
heroes."[4] Most of us, of course, just do not get the

4. Anouilh, *Cahiers, 26,* 7.

joke —our own joke—and when confronted with our
derisory image, we shrink in a huff and attach it to the
other fellow. This was the reaction of Anouilh himself early in his career, and it may well have been an
inevitable one; for how can one expect a young artist
to take himself any way but seriously? The outcome
was that in each of the early pieces a single, fully
drawn, intensely live, sterling hero was put on display
before a supporting cast of paste. In other words, the
young playwright tended to create one flesh-and-blood
character—himself—and to turn the rest of the world
to caricature.[5]

Obviously a strategy like this was an open invitation
to attack. Serge Radine, writing fairly early, went so
far as to describe Anouilh's theatre as basically oriented about the author's egocentricity and failure to
appreciate others.[6] Even Anouilh's admirers have con-
ceded that he wrote no real drama—i.e. drama of conflict—until *Antigone*, when at last he threw off his
blinders and created on stage two equally viable individuals with clashing points of view. True, the conflict
in these first works was smouldering *within* each protagonist, but even interior conflict must be objectified
in hurtling characters if it is to be played out on a
stage, and not on a couch.

If this early dichotomy between character and caricature had its weaknesses, it also had advantages. The

5. The world was sometimes depicted by lifeless agents rather
than by what may properly be called caricatures. Similar to the
flattest of the classical confidants, these agents had only one function:
to elicit response from the hero. Philippe in *L'Hermine* offers an
excellent illustration, his lines all being, roughly, "Frantz! What's
wrong? What are you thinking?" See esp. *PN*, pp. 45–49.

6. Radine, *Anouilh, Lenormand, Salacrou: Trois Dramaturges à
la recherche de leur vérité* (Geneva, 1951), p. 17.

principal theme in the initial works was, in the great romantic tradition, the hero's isolation from and superiority to society. What better way to dramatize such isolation than by setting off the two groups on different planes? How better to dramatize the hero's superiority than by interiorizing only him and dispatching everyone else to pasteboard? Besides, there was something neat and clean about this early approach. Every figure was catalogued; the spectator always knew how to react, whom to take seriously, and whom (paraphrasing the dramatist's own formula) to dismiss with the contemptuous smile one accords a puppet.[7] In fact, it was this very dichotomy that Anouilh relied upon to establish his caricatures. A basic law of the stage is that a creature is viable only to the extent that other characters bother to imbue him with life: by taking one another seriously, characters create an atmosphere of psychological realism, and by refusing to behold one another as human beings, they turn themselves into puppets or symbols. It was really the protagonist, then, who "created" the early caricatures simply by reacting to them as such or by so labeling them before their entrances. Hence in *Le Bal des voleurs* Lady Hurf, quite a clown in her own right, managed nevertheless to reinforce other caricatures by calling her brother an "imbecile," her wards "madcaps," and everyone else "marionettes" or "puppets."[8]

Less obvious advantages were gained by juxtaposing

7. Anouilh, *Cavalcade d'amour* (Paris, 1941), p. 33.

8. We note, in passing, a corollary formula obtained in these early efforts: the single living character could not endure the barest attack on his own dignity, and tended to behave with unremitting earnestness.

these two kinds of stage creatures. The meeting of hero and marionette frequently brought out the humor of a situation. Slapstick routines, as we know, may need a puzzled or scandalized bystander to catalyze laughter in an audience. If humor arises from some deviation from an established norm, then when that norm is physically present in the form of a sane onlooker the deviation is more extreme. The audience automatically identifies with the onlooker and is thus drawn right into the situation. Æsthetic distance shrinks, the gulf between normal and extravagant looms wider, and laughter intensifies. In Anouilh's early plays the same principle operated. Caricatures were rarely set loose on stage without a neutral character to serve as a norm and a point of identification. The result was some hilarious scenes, and some terribly poignant scenes as well. One of the most celebrated moments in Anouilh's theatre occurs during such a juxtaposition: while Orphée and Eurydice are lost in the transports of their new and (what the author obviously intends us to consider) pure love, Eurydice's mother begins carrying on downstage with a former suitor. By their lies and play-acting, which are directed as much to themselves as to one another, the elderly marionettes refute the very notion of love. Their exchanges, to be sure, are funny, but the spectator cannot laugh. His eyes pass swiftly from the clowns to the lovers—who have overheard everything—and he feels a tension as the caricatures all but annihilate the creatures of flesh.

In each of these early plays the character of depth was invariably a youth, and the world of marionettes surrounding him was sure to contain a parent or two. "He has become a man, that is to say, the caricature of

what he once was"; "They always say that it's from a
worm that the butterfly is formed; with men it is the
butterfly who turns into a worm." Actually, these lines
were written by Montherlant,[9] but the vision they convey was for fifteen years Jean Anouilh's. So ingrained
and pervasive was the sentiment that it once led
Robert Kemp (who until his death a few years ago,
was Paris' most influential theatre critic) to fume,
"After your fifties you are not totally ignoble according to M. Anouilh. You are farce. You are grotesque."[10] And when one pauses to consider a play
like *Eurydice,* with its father who clearly symbolizes
the degradation of man by time, one is forced to agree.
Of course, Anouilh eventually did evolve, and shortly
before he reached his own fifties, he began caricaturing
the younger (albeit new) generation and displaying
a trifle more tolerance toward grownups, of which
group he was now a literal if not an altogether en-
raptured member. *La Foire d'empoigne* has probably
marked the close of the cycle: young d'Anouville (*né*
d'Assonville in a primitive version), by his words and
acts, is a brutal caricature of the heroes of yore; by his
name, he is a caricature of their creator.

The fact is that the puppets eventually took over
the stage. And as they were choking the life out of
Anouilh's flesh and blood heroes, the distinctions and
techniques of the past were superseded. With no more
three-dimensional people to rely upon to establish his
caricatures, the playwright turned to another means:
spontaneous generation. It was simple: no labels, no
intricate preparations, just a clown charging onto the

9. *La Reine morte,* III.6; I.3.
10. Robert Kemp, *La Vie du théâtre* (Paris, Albin Michel, 1956),
p. 93.

set and screaming (with the appropriate signs), "I am
a jackass!" The audience got the point. All Anouilh
had to do was to handle the entrance properly. First
impressions in the theatre are just about as crucial as
they are in real life; for if that noble aversion to modi-
fying them is somewhat diminished in the auditorium,
there is also less time in which to do so. Thus we see
the dramatist deftly generating his caricatures from
the first sounds they utter on stage, allowing them to
enter on an embarrassing *quid pro quo* and letting
their opening lines reveal their point of ridicule at its
extreme. One may compare, for example, the first
exchanges of the duchess in *L'Hermine* with those of
Léocadia's duchess: both women are extravagant, but
only the second is presented in startling, colorful terms
from her opening lines.

Once the plays were inhabited only by puppets,
Anouilh altered his entire concept of character. Earlier, we saw him rejecting the orthodoxies of dramatic
form; now we again see him striking out in the direction of greater freedom as he throws off the rule of consistency of character. The law that a character should
not change in the course of a work of art is a persistent
one, traceable via Boileau all the way back to Horace,
who stated it as simply as anyone: "Let Achilles always
be Achilles." Of course the thinking behind the rule
is quite false. Four centuries ago Montaigne, one of
Anouilh's favorite writers, remarked: "We are all
framed of flaps and patches and of so shapeless and
diverse a contexture that every piece and every moment plays its part. And there is as much difference
found between us and ourselves as between ourselves
and others" (*Essais,* III, 1). More recently, Dostoevsky
and professional psychologists have so thoroughly dis-

credited the notion that it has all but disappeared from modern fiction.

Dramatists, too, since the turn of the century, have attempted to free the stage of fraudulently cohesive characters. Reacting less to classic canons than to the dulling parade of reasonable bourgeois figures from nineteenth-century dramas, Strindberg, in his preface to *Miss Julia,* formally rejected the notion of the "immobility of the soul." Pirandello, also, denied that human beings were consistent—or, to be more accurate, it was his characters who said they rejected this notion, and then went on to display themselves with traditional cohesiveness: even the schizophrenic Henry IV remains essentially true to his "selves"; and the father of *Six Characters,* while refusing to be typed on the basis of a single act, still appears to be "of a piece." More recently, Jean-Paul Sartre announced that he had abandoned the bourgeois "theatre of character" for the existentialist "theatre of action," in which the characters would define themselves before us—and they do, with as much logic and consistency as the bourgeois ever did.

The truth is that, much word rattling to the contrary, twentieth-century stage characters are remarkably cohesive, and many respectable literary figures believe they should be. The wise Colette once complimented the fledgling Anouilh for maintaining precisely such consistency in his marionettes.[11] Moreover, shortly after the Liberation, just as Anouilh was liberating his own approach to character, fellow play-

11. "Verisimilitude demands only—as in musical compositions—that the hero be symphonically faithful to the adopted tonality," she wrote in 1935 in praise of *Y'Avait un Prisonnier.* In *La Jument noire, Oeuvres, 10* (Paris, Flammarion, 1949), 240.

wrights were still repeating the formula. "Theatre is founded on the coherence of character," said Montherlant, for example, "life is founded on its incoherence."[12] Certainly there was nothing intellectually original about Anouilh's new approach; but it was, in terms of stage practice, something of an innovation.

And just how does Anouilh dramatize the inconsistency of man? Without a word of explanation or theory, he simply runs the gamut of *theatrical* presentation, exhibiting a person one instant as a puppet and the next as a prince, transposing him into and out of caricature with the ease and artifice of a showman. Sometimes the modulations occur logically, as when the puppet recalls his childhood or comes face to face with death, but more often they follow no other dictates than those of dramatic rhythm. Occasionally, a shift in register forces us to gaze into the soul of a marionette. Georges Neveux put it this way: "As if, during a puppet show, the puppeteers dropped the dolls, raised their heads in front of the set, and suddenly began playing with their own bare faces."[13] Then again, a man of substance may crumble before us into caricature—a less upsetting reversal, as we behold it often in daily life.

This was a new and disconcerting technique, and there was something inevitable about the bewilderment and hostility it provoked in the public. Neveux, in the brisk sentence quoted above, was describing the brutal fourth-act bedroom scene of *La Valse des toréadors*. Unfortunately, he went right on to echo the prevalent objection of critics: "Either the whole play

12. Henry de Montherlant, *Théâtre* (Paris, Gallimard, 1954), p. xx.
13. *Arts* (Jan. 25, 1952).

should have been written this way, or else this particular scene should have maintained the tone of the rest
of the play." The point is that the characters were, in
effect, unstable; no longer could they neatly be tagged
"hero" or "puppet." Hence spectators were no longer
sure how to react to them: Who was real? Who was
make-believe? Questions of "theat-reality," so popular
among today's scholars, seem particularly relevant to
Anouilh's half-floating world. Grossvogel, for one, has
constructed ingenious but highly debatable categories
whereby some of Anouilh's people would be physically
real while spiritually unreal, and some of them would
be the other way round.[14] Not a few theorists maintain that as soon as a spectator laughs at a creature,
he can no longer believe in that creature's existence
as a human being (Bergson's notion), or that he must
at least reduce the creature to a drastically inferior
plane (Baudelaire's). But theorizing of this sort, however stimulating, can only lead one away from the
texts and into the realm of personal abstraction. Let
us simply conclude that Anouilh's present-day characters are fluid, caricatural transpositions of human
beings into stage beings, and that from time to time
they are able to reassume their humanity and to project this humanity onto the spectator. To illustrate:

L'Hurluberlu was Anouilh's most successful play
of the last decade. To some observers its hero was
nothing but a clown, a coarse caricature of the reactionary army officer. But to others (including the
dramatist himself) he was obviously much more. Actor
Paul Meurisse once told how the playwright, as direc-

---

14. David I. Grossvogel, *The Self-Conscious Stage in Modern
French Theatre* (New York, 1958).

tor, helped him to recreate the complex personality of the General: "He has his own particular method. By little bits that he drops to pick up others. You could say that he was trying to illuminate every aspect, every facet of the characters. Not as if he were their father, but as if the characters of his comedy were being shown on the stage detached from him, in their own reality."[15]

As Argan began *Le Malade imaginaire,* so the General opens this comedy of character, by reviewing at length his past life. But unlike Molière's hero, the General seems fairly intelligent. While recounting his youthful role in a cabal against the regime, he spices his remarks with cynicism and self-deprecation. Even as he starts denouncing the "worms," those scoundrels who have eaten away at the beautiful fruit of France, he presents a logical and coherent argument for rigor and grandeur, and opposes it to the current tenor of facility. It is not until several moments later that we, together with the doctor, his interlocutor, come to realize that the General has an *idée fixe,* an area of total blindness: more than a mere reactionary, more than a misanthrope, he truly believes he can change the world, that he really *is* organizing a conspiracy. But it is already too late for us to dismiss the fellow as a mere puppet: we have been hoodwinked into believing in him, or at least in a part of him.

The actual caricature of this man is limited to two distinct areas: his political conspiring and his exaggerated sense of honor. In the former his split from

15. *Les Nouvelles littéraires* (Feb. 5, 1959). Michel Bouquet, interpreter of Bitos and other key roles in Anouilh's plays, has attested to much the same thing, in *Arts,* No. 836 (1961).

reality, immediately obvious from the very nature of the conspiracy, is accentuated by some farcical acting. For example, in disclosing his machinations to the doctor, he delivers the simple line, "I am conspiring," by abruptly lowering his voice, looking about suspiciously, and striking an absurdly mysterious pose. And when the conspirators hold their first council, they also assume the storybook spy posture. As for the hero's outdated concept of honor, it is ridiculed not only by the head-butting milkman and the fisticuffing Mendigalès but by the General himself: sporadically and compulsively, he lunges for his sabers on the wall—his only response to injury, real or imagined. Sporadically, too, he loses all control of his temper:

> THE GENERAL: If one day you were seduced by another man, would you be unfaithful to me?
> AGLAE, *neatly:* No.
> THE GENERAL: Why?
> AGLAE: Because I swore I'd be faithful.
> THE GENERAL, *explodes suddenly:* You are nothing but an impudent flea. Damn it all, I'll show you who I am! Do you expect me to sit back and swallow your pill?
> AGLAE: What pill? I've just told you I'll never be unfaithful.
> THE GENERAL: Because you swore you wouldn't, blast it? Do you think a man worthy of the name will go off into the rain, hiding under an umbrella like that? You've given your word! Well here's one man who doesn't give a damn about your word. I want you never to be unfaithful to me because you love me.   [*HU,* pp. 134–35]

How puzzling it is to compare the General's outburst

with the words uttered by another of Anouilh's bearish heroes in a painfully similar moment:

> COLOMBE: . . . But it's not because of any oath
> that I'm your wife, you silly darling. It's be-
> cause I love you.
> JULIEN, *shouts:* No! I don't want you to be my
> wife because you love me! What difference does
> it make to me that you love me? Tomorrow
> you can stop loving me. I want you to be my
> wife, always, because you've sworn it.
>
> [*PB*, p. 191]

When, in *L'Hurluberlu,* the scatterbrained General
is not playing the fool, he is apt to be radiating lucid-
ity, shrewdness, and wit: he pommels his spinster sister
with sarcasm, he plies his daughter and her fiancé with
irony, he predicts the waning of his son's respect, and
so forth. In the third act he begins a particularly
rending scene with his wife with these words: "I know
there's something grotesque about me. My temper and
selfishness annoy you, I know. They don't always make
things easy for you, nor enjoyable. I have principles,
and that's a virtue. But I'm given to pushing my principles off on others. You see, I'm lucid. I'm a wounded
bear. A man doesn't change" (*HU,* pp. 129–30). A
trite maneuver, this, and yet always so poignant. The
clown admits to his lady, "I know I'm just a clown,
but . . .": the motley has slithered to his feet, leaving
the man naked, alone, pathetic. And we immediately
realize that if *L'Hurluberlu* was the hit of two seasons,
it was because it was both funny *and* moving, because
the author knew just when and how to shut off the
caricature and turn on the soul.

The rest of the cast follow any number of courses. A few characters are simple gags and nothing more. Such would be the milkman or Tante Bise, puppets who may be equated with the rude and intolerant masses or with the sexually obsessed old maid, and who, beyond this, have absolutely no existence. Others, while remaining essentially caricatures, are permitted an occasional trenchant remark: the General's eldest daughter, Sophie, for example, ex-enamorata of Urbain Gravelotte and Jean-François-Marie Piedelièvre, worshiper and wailer of Mendigalès—a *femme fatale* who in one breath resolves to kill herself, become a nun, save lepers, and go on the stage, and who in the very next breath thrusts some ugly truths in the face of her stepmother. Other characters may begin as caricatures only to develop into fierce antagonists of the hero. Such would be Mendigalès himself, introduced as the affable patriot whose industrialist father saved France by turning out soft cement for the Germans, and who later spiritually and physically knocks the General off his feet. Still another member of the cast, the curate, first appears as an ordinary sort of minor character, lapses for a while into clownishness, and then rises to heights of wisdom by telling the General how to handle his woman. By and large, the caricatures are established instantly and effortlessly. Typical is the pot merchant Ledadu's entrance on a quid pro quo: overhearing one of the General's military metaphors, he lunges into the midst of a delicate conversation, sounding the charge on an imaginary bugle, brandishing his cane, and crying, "Worm!" And as everyone falls into caricature, a constant and shifting war of mockery is waged on stage: father mocks daughter, daughter mocks father, Mendigalès mocks everyone,

General mocks conspirators, etc. Truly, in this play, as in traditional farce, the blind inveigle the blind.

One very basic question remains: why bother modulating the worlds of marionette and man in the first place? If Anouilh regards caricaturing as theatre's intellectual game par excellence (and excels in the game besides), if the device has enabled him to convey his vision of life honestly yet inoffensively, why has he not created something of a puppet theatre, one close to *Ardèle?* Because theatre, good theatre at least, must do more than precipitate laughter, no matter how manly or how intellectual; it must do more than transpose life to a superior plane. It must communicate that life, and do it with intensity: it must move us. And we are simply not moved by caricatures; we are moved by people.

But the playwright is not content to remain long in the same register. After all, we are in the theatre. The æsthetic distance may have been lessened, permitting us to lose ourselves for a moment in the plights of the characters, but we must not forget that they are characters, that we are supposedly also savoring the whole transposition of life into drama. Inconsistency? We believe not. All that is required of the spectators is a perceptual dexterity, a willingness to play with the author, to feel one minute and to savor the next, a willingness to match this fellow who into his playwriting has put as much playing as writing.

4.   Self-Dramatizing

"This little comedy is getting longish."[1]
Toward the end of a farce we sometimes hear a creature tattling on his own theatricality. "This scene is ridiculous!"[2] says another, and we should like to brush away his words as more of the same idle preciosity. But we cannot. When André Bitos cries, "This scene is ridiculous!" he means just that. More than self-conscious, Bitos is theatre-conscious: he is dramatizing his very existence; he is his own spectator. Everyone, in fact, self-dramatizes in Anouilh's world, and, to varying degrees, everyone's behavior and thinking reflect the practice.

Attacking this trait from the extreme, where its qualities are most clearly discernible, we run into a few people whose histrionics border on hysteria: "Léon! She has killed Léon! . . . Léon assassinated! Léon dispatched by the inlaws! The moment is prodigious! The instant is unique! . . . I can see the blood of Léon flowing. He is perishing at the hands of a blackguard. And we are here like a Greek chorus, powerless, livid, mute . . ." (*NPN*, pp. 247–48). The chorus here, perched atop a sofa and muffled in an oversized tuxedo, is Lucien of *Roméo et Jeannette*. Before him, dangling from the hands of one of the

1. *PB*, pp. 146, 533.
2. *PN*, p. 93; *PG*, p. 458.

characters, is Léon, sister Jeannette's late pet chicken. Ten years later, Ornifle, who has just passed out from fright at the click of an unloaded pistol, recovers in time to see his illegitimate son (and would-be assailant) collapse in turn—from malnutrition. Ornifle leaps upon his huge canopied bed and bellows to his entourage, whom he has tricked into believing that he is dying from a rare coronary disease, "Great! Him too! He's having a heart attack! It's hereditary! Destiny is upon us. We're playing out a Greek tragedy!" (*PG,* p. 311).

Underneath the humor, which is simply a humor of exaggeration, we can sense in these two passages the principal effect of self-dramatizing: it brings vitality and dash to the dialogue. Maeterlinck once situated his plays clear at the other end of the spectrum. Dealing with undramatic, drab, inarticulate souls, he sometimes put his audiences to sleep. Anouilh, on the contrary, peoples his plays with histrionic characters —hams, show-offs, posers, like Lucien or Ornifle—and they prod and dominate his audiences. Shakespeare and Edmond Rostand did the same thing, said T. S. Eliot in his essay "Rhetoric and Poetic Drama" (1919).[3] According to Eliot, when Cyrano delivers his famous tirade on noses, he is observing himself as a dramatic figure, just as anyone may do in situations he particularly enjoys, and he derives from this awareness a gusto that is rare on the modern stage. Eliot went on to note that naturalist playwrights avoid such consciously dramatic characters for fear of their seeming less real to the audience. Anouilh, of course, is no naturalist, and he must have realized that this very

3. *Selected Essays* (London, 1946), pp. 40–41.

gusto and vitality would enable his characters, flimsy caricatures though they be, to bolt across the footlights and spring to life in the hearts of the spectators. "I've rarely been bored at one of Maxime's parties. He has an astonishing sense of theatre," says one of the hecklers of poor Bitos, and his words are applicable to all of Anouilh's characters.

The words may even be applicable to the playwright himself. Admittedly, Anouilh's sense of drama in his own life is a matter of conjecture: for a man of the theatre he has been outrageously clever at keeping his affairs inviolate. It is our impression, though, that histrionic sensitivity must run very deep in a person who began writing plays at the age of ten (and versions of *Cyrano*, at that); who since his mid-twenties has earned a living exclusively from the theatre (at least so he claims, despite the occasional flashing of a film credit bearing his name); who now directs his own and others' plays; who at home collects miniature historic stages; who has married two actresses and fathered at least one (at the present writing two of his children have not yet broken into their teens); and who in interviews has dropped such remarks as: "I can't even go to a funeral any more without saying to myself in the midst of the lamentations, 'That one is lying—my God, is she awful.' "[4] We suspect that Jean Anouilh is forever at the theatre, and especially so when he stumbles inside one of his own histrionic characters.

If such characters have brought life and vigor to Anouilh's universe, they have brought irony, too. A person who dramatizes himself is often nothing more

4. Anouilh, in *Paris-Match* (June 13, 1959), p. 97.

than a play-actor; he is a counterfeit or, as Sartre would say, "inauthentic."[5] Two groups of people are particularly prone to this theatrical form of deceit: politicians and professional actors.

Politicians, for Jean Anouilh, *are* play-actors, or, rather, they have been play-actors since the French Revolution. Mirabeau advises Robespierre-Bitos to master the tragedian's art; after all, he says jauntily, they *are* in the theatre. Napoleon parades himself throughout *La Foire d'empoigne* as an opportunist devoid of any conviction, a soulless actor who bases his every move on the impression it will create. Any number of his lines convey this mentality: "I have only one thing on my mind now, my foot on the gangplank of this rotten tub about to whisk me off forever: and that's to bring off my exit. Not that desert island business: that's just a curtain raiser with third-rate actors. I mean my *real* exit, down there, all alone. In plain language I must croak with style" (*PC*, p. 369).

Professional actors, Anouilh implies, are professional liars, and their working day is never over. In the first act of *Colombe* Julien promises his wife that upon his return from the army, they will have scenes of violent outburst and reconciliation as "real" lovers do. Later in the play, after Colombe has become an actress, they actually do have such a scene, and it occurs, quite appropriately, in her dressing room. Julien accuses Colombe of infidelity. Colombe denies the charge. Colombe weeps. Colombe countercharges. Colombe ridicules. Colombe is so carried away by the text that she stumbles on her own embellishments. The little actress is overindustrious, perhaps, but she is young

5. See esp. "Intimité," in *Le Mur* (Paris, 1939).

and not nearly so contemptible as her elder colleagues; for the continual exercising of this art, Anouilh would say, eventually corrodes the actor's soul and reduces him to a hollow shell of gestures and lies. And this disdain for theatre people is not just a pose. Anouilh really feels it, and has said as much in his "Lettre à une jeune fille qui veut faire du théâtre."[6] Writing several months after his own daughter, Catherine, had made her stage debut in *Cécile,* and about a year and a half before the secret leaked out of his marriage to actress Charlotte Chardon, from the cast of *Bitos,* the playwright found very little to admire in the acting profession. In fact, under a screen of precious and witty circumlocutions, his attitude was one of hostility, even revulsion, before people who live to lie—not for love, lucre, or power, but for the mere pleasure of lying:

> "Go on!" said the wise old priests of the seventeenth century. "Give absolution to *those* souls! To which of their souls, anyway! And for which of their sins? For the real—and harmless—sins of their lives? Or for the false, horrible sins which every evening they would mimic so well that they would actually turn white in the face, perspire, and scream?"
>
> The devil himself must be baffled, and must quarter them in some sort of infernal theatre where they eternally play parts amidst false flames. I'll wager you that even there they'll have found a way to shake off their real pains and to feign others.[7]

6. *Elle* (Jan. 21, 1955).

7. In *La Petite Molière* Anouilh portrayed Armande Béjart as an evil woman who seduced Molière merely to become an actress. He wrote the part (asserted Gabriel Marcel in *Les Nouvelles littéraires,*

This is certainly not the first time actors have been indicted by a man who bakes them their daily bread. And yet it is one of the most perplexing instances. Almost wed to the stage from his youth, Anouilh has conceived an aversion for stage people; insatiable in his love of theatre when it is held within the playhouse, he abhors theatre when it escapes its confines and invades public life. Frenchmen nurtured on Molière know how the Alcestes are forever doomed to fall in love with the Célimènes, and along comes Jean Anouilh with a burning love for theatre, shouting, "But I'm a light-hearted, easygoing fellow—since I'm in show business,"[8] and we can only smile with him. The one trace of French *clarté* in all the madness has been the sudden extinction of a budding French starlet: Charlotte Chardon.

While histrionic characters may radiate life and irony, they do not necessarily mean good theatre. Early in his career Anouilh was much too direct and clumsy in his handling of self-dramatization. Like Molière or Salacrou, the youthful Anouilh probably once hoped to become a writer of serious drama. His first performed work, *L'Hermine*, skirted melodrama for its entire three acts. On six occasions the principals literally dropped to their knees in paroxysms of feeling. A year later the emotional plummeting deepened as Jézabel and Marc, together on stage for a good part of the play, scarcely managed to confront each other at eye-to-eye level. The protagonists of these early

---

Nov. 9, 1959) expressly for his own daughter, Catherine. (Anouilh's daughter has also played the title role in *Cécile*, Marguerite in *Ornifle,* and Nathalie in a revival of *Ardèle*.)

8. Preface to *Becket,* in *L'Avant-Scène,* No. 282–83 (1963).

plays were so obsessed by the theatre that they could
be accused of overplaying their very existence. Exchanges like the following were quite common:
" 'What's wrong? You're as white as a ghost.' 'That's
exactly the question the minor character asks in a
melodrama' " (*PN*, p. 108). At the climactic moment
of *L'Hermine,* after Frantz has escaped the wiles of
the police and is at last ready to flee with Monime,
without warning she suddenly rejects him. No longer
will she believe that he has slain her aunt to protect
the purity of their love; she accuses him of murdering
the old woman for her money. And Frantz's reaction?
"Oh, this scene, it's just too stupid . . ." (ibid., p. 119).

Anouilh was in his early twenties when he wrote
these plays; subsequently, he has rarely been so inept
as to inject self-consciousness at really crucial moments. At best, it can reinforce the spectator's own
awareness of the drama in front of him, but more
likely it will detract from an otherwise forceful scene:
how is the viewer to lose himself in the struggles of
these creatures when they don't even lose themselves?
Awareness is indeed painful when it undermines
flights of emotion. Eliot pointed this out in the essay
mentioned above, noting that Rostand's characters
dramatize themselves to excess, whereas Shakespeare's
know when and how to transcend themselves.

Since the last "pièces noires," Anouilh's people
have learned to rise above hollow histrionics. The
writer has been less and less inclined to let his characters dramatize themselves, save for displays of ridicule and irony. This is in keeping with a broad movement in his dramaturgy toward understatement and
suggestion. For some fifteen years now, shouting and
histrionics have been relegated for the most part to

moments of gaiety or derision; really lethal lines are delivered sotto voce, the players often not even daring to look at one another. It is possible that Anouilh has found that he could exploit melodrama much more effectively if he subjected it to irony and to his prodigious sense of humor. It is equally possible that he has come to look upon blustering and raging with contempt, even with repugnance, and to behold true drama in the muffled barbarities of restrained dialogue. In any event, the trend reflects an emerging mastery of the medium. In fact, Anouilh shows so cavalier a confidence in the impact of certain key lines that he is nearly willing to scuttle them. The effects are well worth the risks, for the impact is more disturbing when, amidst noisy histrionics, the vital blows are merely suggested. The spectator, no longer a passive agent assailed by a stream of purportedly significant lines (as he is during a Sartre play, let us say), has instead the impression that he is discovering on his own Anouilh's beautiful and ugly truths.

Although Anouilh may have checked the runaway histrionics of his characters early in his career, it was already too late for his dramaturgy not to have been vastly and permanently affected. One outgrowth in particular has given an unusual stamp to his writings. A man conscious of the dramatic values of his position is by extension aware of himself in all circumstances; he enjoys a certain detachment from himself and his surroundings and, as a detached observer, can freely comment on what is occurring within himself and without. Long after these creatures had stopped overdramatizing, they continued to exteriorize—that is, to talk about what was taking place on stage, to interpret their own or one another's behavior. A remarkable

proportion of an Anouilh dialogue may be consumed
by this involuted dramatizing; in fact, one sometimes
has the impression that a few seconds of action can
lay the seed for an entire act of commentaries. This is
precisely what happened in *Roméo et Jeannette*.

Critics have been rather harsh in their appraisals of
this piece. Just about everyone has decried the implau-
sibility of the humdrum and truehearted Frédéric's
falling in love with a crass wench like Jeannette, and
on the eve of his wedding besides. As the play is essentially a melodrama, relieved only by passing gibes from
Jeannette's drunken housemates, this incredibility is
most unfortunate. Perhaps it was to escape it that the
London production shifted the play's locale to Ireland,
where (as an English critic scoffed) "anything is possible."[9] What is truly surprising, though, is that
Anouilh permitted his lovers to remain conscious of
all that is incongruous in their situation and even to
expatiate upon it. Indeed, the couple is continuously
and acutely aware of *everything*, and never at a loss
to say so.

At times they certify simple things: Frédéric grasps
Jeannette's wrist and she cries out, "That's right, hurt
me! Twist my arm the way you did before" (*NPN*,
p. 301). Jeannette's line is a natural one, and it neatly
reinforces for the audience Frédéric's brutality. With
equal felicity, the practice is sometimes exploited for
humor: a character will mimic, deny, or grossly mis-
interpret a particular piece of stage business that the
spectator himself has already witnessed and understood (Jeannette spews a string of insults and her
father discusses the girl's inner goodness). In earlier

9. Walter Allen, in the *New Statesman and Nation* (Sept. 10,
1949).

plays Anouilh's characters—in the great Racinean tradition of "Seigneur, vous changez de visage"—were
wont to lend a hand to nearsighted spectators by
signaling one another's facial changes: "You're sad,
Frantz. Do you think I don't know why? You jumped.
You moved your lips" (*PN*, p. 55). But by the time he
wrote *Roméo et Jeannette*, the playwright had learned
not only that scowls and twitches were obvious to view-
ers without commentary but, more important, that
intense and shifting emotions could not be established
or communicated merely "from the outside," by ma-
nipulations of hands and faces.

On a somewhat higher plane, exteriorizing may be
a crystallizing device, designed to clarify for the spectator elements that have been either too diffuse or
only implicit in the stage action. In theory, such
focusing also helps the characters: it enables them to
rise and discuss their dilemma with added force and
eloquence. Too often, however (at least in *Roméo et
Jeannette*), the device miscarries and the exteriorizing
degenerates into flat, gratuitous restatements of what
the spectator can plainly see before him: "You don't
say a word now. You're standing near me, I can hear
you breathing in the dark" (*NPN*, p. 272), or, "I already left once, and it was for good. Even now I'm
talking to you from the other end of the world. Our
very meeting was that extra little minute destiny sometimes grants, once the dice have been thrown. Our
two trains are picking up speed now, they're crossing"
(ibid., pp. 335–36). Just as often, the device leads to
sensationalism and bombast: "Who is she, that woman,
all in black, with her low forehead, her bulging eyes,
her proper airs? Who brought her here with her
widow's hat?" (ibid., p. 249). Before long, the char-

acters turn their third eye inward to analyze their own souls. Admittedly, this is hallowed practice, close to the traditional psychologizing of French theatre. But whereas Racine's lovers may probe the growth and deviations of passion in tirades of supreme poetic beauty, Frédéric and Jeannette do so before one another patiently, clumsily, prosaically: "I'm weak and cowardly now, as before. Once again I've become lies, disorder, sloth" (ibid., p. 346). At worst, we are assailed by clusters of lackluster judgments:

LUCIEN: You're lucky. She's a good woman. Tiresome, but good. *He leaves.*

FREDERIC: Poor fellow! He must have suffered a lot.

JULIA: He is odious.

FREDERIC: He's nice.

JULIA: Oh you, the strong man! Always stronger than everyone else. Everything makes you laugh, you excuse everything . . . [Ibid., p. 231]

The inevitable question is whether all this exteriorizing, judging, and characterizing makes for good theatre. One's first reaction is probably negative; for as everyone knows, drama should demonstrate, not elucidate. Even novelists no longer explain, and prefer instead to let characters establish themselves through their acts. Still, there is nothing fundamentally wrong with the technique. The foregoing illustrations, limited to one of the poorer plays, naturally point to various weaknesses: when practiced to excess, exteriorizing interrupts a play's movement, it undermines the emotional impact, it belabors points which the audience can and should grasp unassisted. But when the writer employs the technique with discretion—and Anouilh certainly has in more recent works[10]—it leads to a richness and subtlety of characterizing that are overpowering. Actions may speak louder than words, but an occasional flash of rhetoric may be more illuminating. Some two hundred years ago Rousseau carped at the talkiness of French drama. There are more words than action on the French stage, he wrote in *La Nouvelle Héloïse,* and this is so not because Frenchmen talk more than they act, but because they value what a man says more than what he docs. Fortunately for Rousseau's own posterity, he was right. And it may well be fortunate for Anouilh's posterity that he has maintained the French tradition of a theatre of language.

Quite a few of the behavior patterns of Anouilh's people arise from this same dramatic acuteness. An individual aware of himself as a performer quite understandably becomes concerned with his staging; he needs to "set the scene" properly. Hence the characters are prone to jockey one another into prescribed poses before being able to communicate: "Please sit down. It's much better to learn tragic news sitting down. It avoids certain ridiculous gestures" (*YA,* p. 23); or, "How clumsy you are, Julia! You're so stiff and dignified . . . cry, go on, cry. Melt him, break him" (*NPN,* p. 279). Lines of this sort are of negligible value, unless through them some of the hypersensitivity to visual setting is transferred to the audience, or unless they are exploited for humor (as disengaged commentaries on one's surroundings easily are).

A more obvious outgrowth of the self-dramatizing

10. Cf. *PB,* p. 376.

tendency can be seen in the theatrical language that
pervades the dialogues. As Napoleon's words, above,
may have indicated, a man who pictures himself constantly on the stage instinctively picks up a certain
stagy jargon: he thinks in terms of entrances, exits,
curtains, stage effects, and so forth: "What a wonderful entrance she just made for us" (*NPN,* p. 325);
"We'll see. We always see. That's what is marvelous
about the human condition. We cry 'Eureka' five
minutes before we die and the curtain falls on that
comforting word" (*PB,* p. 423); "I'd like to get Colombe across first. You'll make your entrance in the
second set. Repentant son, big-hearted mother—all
we have to do is suggest the scene. I know her, she'll
play it" (ibid., p. 195). This is a shallow device, but a
salutary one. Just as any mystery or ghost-story writer
makes his tales more terrifying by loading them with
words like "bloody," "macabre," and "gruesome," so
has Anouilh, by exploiting the dynamic idiom of the
stage, heightened the theatricality of his plays. Of
course, such a technique can never be more than a
condiment; happily, Anouilh has been equally liberal
with the meat of real dramatic conflict.

The characters' habit of self-dramatizing remotely
affects them in still another way: they tend to regard
all of life as a play and to live it as such. Life is a tale
told by an idiot, said Shakespeare, and Anouilh would
counter—or at least so it would appear on the surface
—that life can be anything from an absurd melodrama
to a fastidiously well-regulated comedy. It is his bitter
and disillusioned heroes who are most apt to call life
a farce: to Frantz impoverished youth is a "sinister
farce" (*PN,* p. 36); General Saint-Pé closes his adventures sighing, "What a farce! It's lugubrious" (*PG,*

p. 207). For politicos of the revolutionary breed, life is a melodrama. The aristocrats, on the other hand, view existence as a comedy of "good" manners. One errs in taking anything too seriously, they say. How much more civilized it is simply to obey the elegant codes of behavior: "Our life has been a frivolous comedy. Let's keep the tone," says Ornifle de Saint-Oignon to his wife (ibid., p. 304). The Count echoes the same refrain to his wife: "We have lived the way people dance: to music, on measured steps, and with grace" (*PB*, p. 471), but two acts later he is ready to end the ballet and struggle gracelessly for a life of happiness with Lucile. Indeed, we are here approaching the heart of Anouilh's world; for life according to him, once one gets beyond the surface, is neither farce nor melodrama nor comedy; it is not a Shakespearean joke played on mankind by wanton or puerile gods. Civilized life is just a willful game of appearances danced by well-mannered hypocrites.[11] It is in this context that the playwright unleashes his spoilsports, his *empêcheurs de danser en rond,* those overly principled individuals who would rebel against the ballet of appearances. And it is against this backdrop that occurs the central conflict between facility and rigor, between liberty and virtue, between accepting life and everything in it by playing the game, and refusing life by literally demanding the ideal. Anouilh's early heroes refused to put on an act: "Don't you know how to play with life?" asked Jeannette, to which Frédéric replied, *no* (*NPN,* p. 336). A year later Médée, in what

11. This same theme of hypocrisy or the mask dominates the group of French playwrights with whom Anouilh is often associated: Molière, Marivaux, Musset.

is generally regarded as Anouilh's pivotal work, dared her partner, "Play the game, Jason, make the gestures, say yes" (ibid., p. 394). And for once a protagonist *did* attempt to build something stable on the appearances of life.

Dramatizing oneself and cultivating one's life as a game or as an art has a further implication: it leads to a sort of æstheticism. All that counts is playing well and playing gracefully; good is equated with beauty, evil with ugliness. The aristocrats, of course, are prone to harbor such an outlook: "Beauty, real beauty, is a serious thing," we hear them saying; "it must be a part of God—if God exists" (*PB,* p. 427). Maxime de Jaucourt, who for years has hated poor Bitos, finally tells him why: "You lacked grace" (*PG,* p. 416)—an explanation which, even in the present context, is somewhat disquieting. But much more important, the heroes themselves embrace this same æstheticism. Jeanne d'Arc has the simplest of credos: "I'm not as learned as you, but I do know that the devil is ugly and that everything beautiful is the work of God" (*PC,* p. 19). Thomas à Becket has a similar code. King Henry accurately surmises that Becket is incapable of lying, because lying appears "inelegant" to him: "Everything that seems to be morality in you is merely æstheticism" (ibid., p. 182). The Archbishop agrees, and later he clarifies: "I like at least one thing, My Lord. To do well what I have to do" (ibid., p. 196). Here again we have a rather disturbing explanation, for the saint who talks in such a manner has obviously been drained not only of religious conviction but of all moral principles. Jacques Guicharnaud tersely analyzes Anouilh's Becket: "As the King's friend . . . what interests him is not debauchery but perfection in debauchery. When the King appoints him Archbishop, all he does is to be the perfect Archbishop."[12] In other words, Becket plays the game. Even Amanda, the heroic little seamstress of *Léocadia*, repeats a similar refrain: "When I do a job, I like to do it well, that's all" (*PR*, p. 339). And so, in fact, does the playwright: "My father was a tailor. He was a simple, genuine man who knew his trade marvelously well and was proud and meticulous in it. Having 'gone astray' in literature, I've always dreamed of being as good a craftsman as he. Even my censors tell me this is so."[13]

That obsessive vision of life as a game generates a whole scheme of values, and many of Anouilh's favorite epithets take on a greater meaning when so viewed. A man who stages his life before others is concerned lest he appear ridiculous. Throughout the works ridicule is one of the most horrid states a person can endure. At the very limit of despair, seeing himself abandoned by the woman for whom he has just committed murder, Frantz weeps, "I am ridiculous. I am absolutely ridiculous. I'm sorry" (*PN*, p. 122). Like many an Anouilh hero, like the playwright himself, who has admitted always having feared ridicule,[14] Ornifle is apt to interrupt a conversation by saying, "Let's stop this! Ridicule gives me an unbearable physical malaise!" "You'll have to learn to bear it," replies his wife; "I've often thought that with a little

---

12. Guicharnaud, *Modern French Theatre from Giraudoux to Beckett* (New Haven, Yale University Press, 1961), p. 124. Leonard Pronko, in *The World of Jean Anouilh* (Berkeley, University of California Press, 1961), concludes, "This sounds curiously like the total lack of faith parading as form, of which Jaspers speaks" (p. 60).

13. Anouilh, in *Opéra* (March 7, 1951).

14. *New York Times* (Oct. 1, 1960), drama section.

less cowardice in the face of ridicule, you would have been a better man" (*PG*, p. 271). The poles in this scheme of values are easily identified: amusement lies at one end, boredom at the other. Marguerite and Colombe, two little birds with a penchant for facility, are forever chirping the words "fun" and "amusing" in the outraged faces of their "boring" companions. Ornifle lectures his son on women: "Be careful not to be boring: it's the one thing they don't forgive us" (ibid., p. 325). The General reviles his wife: "And there's something even stronger than my hatred and my disgust. It's that I'm dying of boredom with you" (ibid., p. 175). No one could receive a greater slap than Villebosse when, already having been designated "ridiculous" in the cast of characters, he is dismissed by the Countess, "You have accomplished the incredible feat of making sin a bigger bore than virtue" (*PB*, p. 374).

This sparring between pleasure and boredom is obviously just another facet of the playwright's single obsessive theme, the conflict between purity and compromise. It was Ornifle who reduced the problem to its simplest alternatives by reciting a little ditty from Péguy: "Le jeune homme bonheur / Voulait danser / Le jeune homme honneur / Voulut passer" (*PG*, p. 332). ["Mr. Happy / Wants to dance. / Mr. Honor / Looks askance."] Ornifle—in fact, every character since Jason—has either known or shown that pleasure and purity don't mix. No one has been able to break the puzzle and be principled without being dreary, pleasing without being depraved. We realize now just how complex the battle lines are in this eternal struggle. The side of ideals, purity, and beauty has allied itself to intransigence, tediousness, and ridicule. The forces of reality, compromise, and ugliness are now associated with indulgence, pleasure, and wisdom. Apparently neither side can win: Anouilh's characters are engaged in a war of attrition, exactly the same sort of war that everyone must wage with life.

5.   The Role

> All the world's a stage,
> And all the men and women merely players:
> They have their exits and their entrances;
> And one man in his time plays many parts,
> His acts being seven ages.

One can only speculate on the extent to which Jean Anouilh was conveying his own sentiments as he translated these lines from *As You Like It*. His adaptations of three comedies by Shakespeare did not appear until 1952, but throughout his career Anouilh seems to have embraced the Shakespearean—that is to say, the Renaissance—view that man is forever playing a part.[1] The idea of role-playing is at bottom just another aspect of the self-dramatizing tendency discussed in the previous chapter; and yet it so deeply pervades the plays, it is so intimately related to their intellectual content, that we may do well to explore it separately.

Role-playing as it appears in Anouilh's works may be approached on three distinct levels. It may be con-

---

1. Montaigne, greatly admired by Anouilh, once expressed a similar thought: "Most of our activities involve comedy. *Mundus universus exercet histrioniam.* All the world practices stage-playing. We must play our part duly, but as the part of a borrowed personage" (*Essays*, III, 10).

sidered, in the first place, as a purely theatricalist device, just another labored cue to the spectator that he
is watching stage figures, each with a precise function
in the script: his role. Any number of lines may be
cited in illustration, such as Médée's, "Quickly, quickly, dear, and you'll have played your part" (*NPN*,
pp. 364–65), or Créon's, "For that's just what I want
you to know: the sordid backstage truths of this drama
in which you're so eager to play a part" (ibid., p. 186).
Depending on one's taste, remarks of this sort may
be adorable, admissible, or abominable. Little else, we
believe, can or need be said. Fortunately, Anouilh
did not stop at this jejune application, but went on to
employ the concept of the role for a second and in-
finitely richer purpose.

Scanning Anouilh's adaptation of *The Winter's
Tale,* we see that he has translated Shakespeare's "Are
you a party in this business?" quite literally into
"Avez-vous un rôle dans cette histoire?" (IV.4). But
a little later, "Wolves and bears, they say, / Casting
their savageness aside have done / Like offices of pity,"
becomes "Il y a eu des loups et des ours, dit-on, qui
dépouillant leur sauvagerie naturelle ont assumé *ce
rôle de bons Samaritains.*"[2] We are on slightly different ground here, for the playwright has thrust someone into a precise, *established* role. Clearly, the good
Samaritan motif does not do too much for the wolves
and bears, but elsewhere in Anouilh's texts the super-
imposed role, whether it be the good Samaritan, the
maudlin romantic, Augustus, Robespierre, or what
have you, is attached to a person as a dramatic metaphor. It immediately illuminates the person to whom

2. *Le Conte d'hiver,* II.3. Italics mine.

it is applied, and, on occasion, the person himself may shed light on the attributed role. In other words, such associations or superimpositions are an easy, tight way of characterizing.

Thus in *L'Hermine* Mr. Bentz casts Frantz into the solid mold of "little Romantic," and subsequently not only he but we of the audience, too, tend to react accordingly to the hero. Ornifle has condemned Mlle. Supo to the barely human role of the devoted old-maid secretary; we and he both follow her ensuing antics with mild contempt. Mlle. Supo, for her part, has cast herself in the role of Ornifle's conscience, whence her eternal reproaches to this man who obviously considers himself to be the reincarnation of Don Juan. Villebosse, the Countess' ridiculous lover in *La Répétition,* is humorously dispatched by Héro as "that graceful natural phenomenon: a man suffering from love" (*PB,* p. 374). The mainspring for the entire play *Pauvre Bitos* is that the protagonist has unconsciously taken himself for a latter-day Robespierre. Maxime, malicious host of the dinner party, realizes this and hence designates Bitos to play the part of Robespierre in the evening's masquerade. The second act is a reinterpretation of Robespierre's career as seen through the eyes of the unconscious Bitos. It is in this play that Anouilh has most fully exploited the role as a dramatic metaphor, a superimposition of two figures, by letting each man's courage and humiliations shed light on the other's rigor and hatred.

Now if we follow one step further this concept of the role as a characterizing frame, we arrive at a theory once advanced by Gaston Baty: that in dramatic literature the type is more of a liberating device than a restrictive one.[3] In effect, Baty's remarks concern the type rather than the role, but the two may easily be equated, and all the more so because Anouilh's roles usually are not filtered down to a Robespierre or even to a Don Juan. More often, the playwright has been content to stamp his people as types, such as the old maid, the decrepit coquette, the coarse soldier, etc. Developing Baty's tenet, we may say that—as Molière and others had already known before Anouilh—the very instant a type is established, it can be developed ad infinitum. The fixed type, then, is actually a short cut for the ever-pressed playwright, a point of reference immediately grasped and assimilated by the audience. More important, it is also a point of departure: it is the raw matter upon which an inventive author can galvanize all the startling effects he chooses. And should the dramatist stray far from familiar recipes, his innovations will impose by their very disparity. To assess Anouilh's exploitation of this technique, we turn to an example.

A woefully eternal role on the American scene is that of the henpecked husband. French husbands, whether because they are impeccable or because their wives' energies are otherwise directed, have a cross of a slightly different form to bear. Evidently it is one pregnant with dramatic possibilities, for it has given substance to much French comic theatre, from medieval farces to contemporary vaudevilles. Jean Anouilh has not been loath to dot his works with discreet "cross-bearers," men whose horns are but a fleeting contin-

3. Gaston Baty and René Chavance, *Vie de l'art théâtral des origines à nos jours* (Paris, 1932), p. 181 (discussing the *commedia dell' arte*).

gency of their dramatic lives—or so it would seem to us heartless spectators. Such are Robert of *Le Rendez-vous de Senlis,* Georges of *Le Voyageur sans bagage,* Messerschmann, M. Tarde, Ludovic, a few counts, General Saint-Pé, Jason, Molière, Charles VI, etc. But on several occasions Anouilh has established characters whose sole function within the play is that of being cuckolds, who sense themselves cast irrevocably as cuckolds, who are primarily cuckolds and nothing but, first, last, and always: cuckolds. Such, for example, are Lucien of *Roméo et Jeannette* and, for one painful scene, Julien of *Colombe.* What are some of the tricks that Anouilh has used in the free development of this fixed type? It certainly is fixed, as Shakespeare pointed out in *The Winter's Tale:*

> Go, play, boy, play: thy mother plays, and I
> Play too, but so disgraced a part, whose issue
> Will hiss me to my grave: contempt and clamour
> Will be my knell. Go, play, boy, play.   [I.2]

Anouilh, champion of rigor, principle, and strenuous effort, has also been willing to play, and to play it easy. In the present case he has approached virtually any adjective to the key word, cuckold, for facile but still quite effective quips. Here are just a few of Lucien's more felicitous qualifiers: "In love I have my diploma. I've made the grade. Doctor Cuckold, that's me!" "You'll make an excellent cuckold . . . a gay cuckold. They're the best. I'm a sad cuckold" ("artsy cuckolds"; "demi-cuckolds"; and so on).[4] Anouilh has, furthermore, exploited that weighty first entrance of a character. Lucien slips on stage while his sister Julia and Frédéric are embracing. "What? Have you

4. *NPN,* pp. 282, 230, 326, 331.

been there all the time?" cries Julia, withdrawing.
Lucien replies, "I'm always there when people kiss,
it's planned that way. Ever since I became a cuckold
I can't take a step without encountering love. . . .
Actually, it's a pleasure. A dark pleasure. I say to myself: 'My! two more who don't have long to go!' "
(ibid., p. 228). And from here on, all his utterances
will grow out of this self-imposed role. He is indeed
a man utterly transfigured by his condition. Critics
have been unanimous in regarding Lucien as a sort of
Greek chorus; and we would note that it is his very
isolation from the play's action which gives weight to
his laments and pronunciamentos. Besides, Lucien's
vitriol projects in even greater relief as the spectator
unwittingly compares him to the typical Unfortunate
French Husband, who, when not downright ridiculous, is noted for flights into philosophic and halcyon
daze. Many regard Lucien as a symbol of the inevitable
disenchantment of love. Their interpretation is interesting, especially in light of a remark made by André
Barsacq, who had been an intimate associate of the
playwright for almost a decade when he staged *Roméo
et Jeannette* in 1946: "Perhaps, indeed, the character
of the brother [Lucien] corresponds most closely to
Anouilh's preoccupations today."[5]

Oddly enough, Julien is consigned to the ill-fated
role not by his wife, Colombe, but by the stage manager, La Surette. In this instance all the "contempt

5. André Barsacq and Pierre-Aimé Touchard, "Roméo et Jeannette," *Le Spectateur* (Feb. 11, 1947). Hubert Gignoux, who in 1946
was completing his study of Anouilh, has since voiced a similar
opinion, in *Arts* (Oct. 27, 1961); and Gabriel Marcel, in *Les Nouvelles
littéraires* (Dec. 12, 1946), called Lucien a "caricatured portrait" of
Anouilh.

and clamour" traditionally associated with the part are crudely dumped upon the bewildered husband. La Surette would reduce this lofty bear to all the sniveling ignominy of the stage cuckold; he would depersonalize the man; he would swallow the individual in the part. Having received a letter from the stage manager saying that his wife is unfaithful, Julien returns on a one-day pass. Conversation begins abruptly: Julien grabs La Surette by the lapels and demands, "Who is he?" The reply is nasty: "There's the rub. That's where it begins, monsieur Julien. It would be too beautiful if you could jump right into the role with certainty. No, it's like everything else, being a cuckold—it's difficult. It's not given to everyone. It has to be learned" (*PB*, p. 254). La Surette continues, alternately elevating Julien's dilemma to cosmic grandeur ("The drama of the cuckold is the drama of man: knowledge"), and reducing his plight to a travesty. Molière's Arnolphe had composed his "Maxims of Marriage"; La Surette derides Julien with the "Axioms for the Cuckold." At the end of the scene Julien is lost and asks what he must do:

> LA SURETTE: First, of all, hide! Always hide, it's another axiom! The cuckold must see without being seen.
> JULIEN: . . . Where?
> LA SURETTE, *opening a closet for him and pushing him inside:* In the closet, like all cuckolds.
> [Ibid., p. 259]

La Surette, leaving Julien hidden in his wife's closet, disappears, resuming his own role as stage manager, shouting, "On stage for Act One!" But, as Robert

Nelson has observed,[6] the act which begins takes place not on stage but in Colombe's dressing room, and its spectators are the actor-characters who gather outside the door.

The third and most significant application of role-playing is philosophical in nature; it centers about problems of sincerity and spontaneity, and its overtones are bleak, sometimes tragic. In the last illustration we saw how La Surette would have submerged Julien in his cuckoldom. Similarly, whenever a character assumes an established role, he risks identifying himself so completely with that role that he loses his individuality. Anouilh seems to imply that the comedy of life contains but a limited number of roles, which must be distributed among all of mankind. It is as if he had accepted and followed to their logical conclusion the views of a Polti that there are only thirty-six dramatic situations possible in human existence.[7] Such determinism is pessimistic and confining; it precludes spontaneity, freshness, originality. Is it not reflected in the following passage?

> You are young, you're disembarking in the country of love; you must feel like an explorer discovering continents . . . Don't protest, it's very nice . . . You'll learn soon enough that the play calls for only two or three parts, two or three eternal situations, and that what gushes so irresistibly from your heart in moments of ecstasy is never anything more than an old, worn-out text, prattled from the dawn of the world by

6. Nelson, *Play within a Play* (New Haven, 1958), pp. 145 ff.
7. Georges Polti, *Les Trente-Six Situations dramatiques* (Paris, 1939).

> mouths long since turned to dust. Rarely does one
> invent anything.   [*PB,* p. 445]

These dismal words are extracted from the seductive
cant of Héro in *La Répétition.* But there are so many
similar speeches in other plays, and the notion is so
often given dramatic form, that inevitably one feels it
is the author himself who is calling human behavior
imitative. One wonders if he isn't extending to all
facets of life La Rochefoucauld's observation that
there are people who would never have fallen in love
had they not first heard about love.

Anouilh has presented both conscious and unconscious role-players—that is, both hypocrites who
crudely usurp a standard role for their own ends, and
dupes who are blind to the imitativeness and the per-
versity of their behavior.

Deliberate counterfeits abound in *Le Rendez-vous
de Senlis.* Georges, the hero, has engaged two professional actors to portray his mother and father before
a young lady. He had assumed that parents were easy
roles to play and is appalled at the stock figures the
actors suggest. After some hard talking, he convinces
the bearded, wrinkled, stooped actor to straighten up
and play a different father, perhaps equally conventional but young and sympathetic. The role-playing
is still to come. Georges' real mother and father now
enter the stage, and it is they who put on the most
fraudulent act by posing as protective parents (they
are protective, but only of their own purses). Robert,
the ugly avatar of Georges' best friend, ashamed at
everyone's hypocrisy (and not, as some would have us
believe, conscious of their illusiveness) grows hyster-
ical and dares the "real" parents to play their roles to

the end. He goads the mother into placing her hand over her heart and the father into acting dignified and quivering his mustache. The parents actually do take his cue, the one beginning *"very 'motherlike'*: Miss . . . I realize this situation is very painful for you as it is for us, but it's a mother who is speaking to you" (*PR,* p. 114). Ironically, these people are true to themselves only when they assume the hypocritical pose.

The conscious role-player, then, is nothing but a hypocrite whose lies are facilitated by the contours of his role. More prevalent in Anouilh's theatre are the unwitting hypocrites, individuals who play out stock parts and ape stock emotions, but who are blithely unaware of their borrowing. The clearest—and least dramatic—exposure of this notion occurs in *Pauvre Bitos.* Frantz Delanoue, a former juvenile delinquent, confronts Bitos, his implacable ex-prosecutor. Delanoue is costumed as the gendarme Merda, about to arrest Bitos-Robespierre. Exacerbated, Bitos exclaims that the youth deserved no pity: "You stole a car and you came up to a post-office window with a revolver in your hand, just as in a bad film." Exactly as in a bad film, agrees Delanoue; an abandoned war orphan, he had been haunting the movies for years and had seen every bad film. He concludes: "I've already been arrested once because I wanted to play robbers. I want to play gendarmes now, to redeem myself. (*He smiles.*) That's all I can do—play" (*PG,* pp. 424–25). With several years' retrospect, Delanoue realizes that, as a youngster, he had been too impressionable; he had witlessly submerged himself in an appealing but foolish role.

On a number of occasions Anouilh has exposed the imitativeness of human behavior. Lieutenant d'Anouville rhapsodizes on heroic death, Lady India pines for idyllic poverty, and both are unconsciously aping the extravagancies of sentimental literature. And both are treated with scorn by the playwright, for they are the world's own caricatures. A delightful moment in *Ornifle* is the reconciliation scene between Marguerite and Fabrice. No sooner has Machetu escorted the wayward filly back to her lover than the two whelps resume bickering, roughly as follows: —Why didn't you wait for me? —Why did you leave? —I thought you were making believe you wouldn't wait. —I thought you were making believe you were leaving. I even counted to a hundred and fifty. —Why a hundred and fifty?

> MARGUERITE, *very dignified:* Normally I only count to a hundred to make you give in, but considering the gravity of the situation, I thought it might be too little. I took pity on you.
>
> FABRICE, *bitter:* A hundred and fifty! So that's your love . . . A girl who loved me wouldn't even have counted!   [Ibid., p. 326]

These are by no means gratuitous caricatures. These are two puppies making their splash in the love puddle, two youths playing at being in love—especially Woman, who plays her part to the hilt: "A woman who loves is so weak!" confides Marguerite; "A woman's broken heart, it's not with words that it can be mended." Anouilh, usually only maddeningly explicit with his stage directions, here becomes downright rabid: "wrings his hands," "leaps," "recoils," "tragic," "hostile," "heroic," etc. And he does so for a purpose: whether spectators or readers, we cannot

help being offended by the pair's histrionics; we instinctively know that these people are not genuine.
Now all the while Ornifle and Machetu have been
watching this little ballet. The not-overly-clever
Machetu sighs, "Aren't they nice!" but Ornifle, with
more acumen, mutters, "Aren't they stupid! And to
say that *this* is love." Several moments later when this
modern Don Juan scores the dearth of true lovers in
today's world, we can be sure that the wretched play-
actors, with their derivative little hearts, are not to be
included.

A variation in minor key of the lovers' quarrel occurs in *L'Orchestre,* in which the entire cast plays at
being temperamental artists. The lovers here are no
longer puppies; they are mature, disillusioned, third-
rate musicians, and their roles call for taut nerves,
tantrums, fits of depression, and even a suicide. What
is bizarre and startling is that these miserable puppets
really play their parts to the end, and as they do, the
spectator is never certain to what extent they are play-
acting and to what extent they are being themselves.
L'Orchestre was a difficult work to stage, we are told.
It must have required extreme subtlety on the part of
the interpreters: they had to sound false and yet be
true; they had to embody the boldest and funniest of
Anouilh's caricatures and yet stab one another with
his grimmest truths.

Many of Anouilh's darker thoughts are linked to
this concept of role-playing. Among them is his tragic
vision of love. Some critics are convinced that there
is no tragedy of love in Anouilh's theatre, for the
simple reason that the playwright does not believe in
love. They are not hard pressed to support the claim.
They merely call attention to the chilling postures of

Ardèle, wherein the passion is reduced to internecine sexual warfare. Or, better yet, they point to *Ardèle's* ironic curtain-raiser, *Episode de la vie d'un auteur.* Here, formal affirmations of love are mocked and negated by their relentlessly farcical context.[8] Many others impute the failure of love in Anouilh's plays to the emotion's inherent egoism: the writer attaches a black meaning to the word, they say, and pounce on one of Poète-Chéri's bons mots: "Love is a gift, the absolute gift of one's self. But everything it gives is for the self" (*PB,* p. 221), or repeat a cynical maxim from *L'Invitation au château:* "We love nothing but our own love, my children, and all our lives we run after this fleeting little image of ourselves" (ibid., p. 144).[9]

But there are still others who would distinguish between what the dramatist truly believes, on the one hand, and what he may happen to see about him, on the other. They detect in the plays an affirmation of love. Some of them stop at the "two-little-brothers" sort of sentiment, the tepid friendship of the boy-and-girl scouts which appears in a number of the works.[10] A few go further. They know that Anouilh's heroes are just as rigorous and demanding in affairs of the heart as they are in every other phase of life, and that the love toward which they strive is a carnal and spiritual love of total communion and total identification

8. See Michel Braspart, in *La Table Ronde* (Dec. 1948).

9. See Pronko, *World of Jean Anouilh,* esp. p. 106; Grossvogel, *Self-Conscious Stage,* esp. p. 169; Jacques Poujol, in the *French Review* (April 1952).

10. See Hubert Gignoux, *Jean Anouilh* (Paris, Temps Présent, 1946), esp. p. 71; Robert de Luppé, *Jean Anouilh* (Paris, Editions Universitaires, 1959), chap. 4.

between the partners.[11] This ideal love is presented clearly enough, though in retrospect, by Jason: "Have you forgotten those days when we did nothing, thought nothing, one without the other? Two accomplices before the harshness of life" (*NPN,* p. 390). Jason continues for several moments, but the rest is superfluous. What he and Médée had known was perfect communion. That such a love is attainable we shall have to take Jason's word. But most of us are probably more inclined to agree with Orphée that no two people can ever maintain this quasi-mystical union; most of us are as lucid as Antigone when she foresaw that her partner would one day laugh at something she did not understand, thereby shattering their perfect union. The failure of this love, then, stems from its idealism.

Anouilh's lovers do more than aspire after the ideal. They idealize their partners, they see them under auras of perfection, and—here lies the mischief—they impose this perfection upon them. The poor partner, beleaguered with a spurious role, has a choice: he may either embrace this role (consciously, like Eurydice, or unconsciously, like Colombe), or else refuse it straightaway. In either case, the role has been legislated from without. The partner can play it for only so long; eventually, his true and imperfect nature will assert itself. Its emergence breaks the illusion and constitutes the tragedy of love.

Given that it is the man who imposes his dream upon the woman, all of this amounts to little more than the dream of Pygmalion, which has haunted mankind for ages—and has been partially realized by many more men than even Denis de Rougemont saw

11. See Edward Owen Marsh, *Jean Anouilh, Poet of Pierrot and Pantaloon* (London, W. H. Allen, 1953), esp. p. 27.

fit to write about. Today's French writers seem particularly fascinated by the theme: Giraudoux skirted
it in *Sodome et Gomorrhe;* Genet plotted his *Balcon*
about it; Salacrou discussed it in *Un Homme comme
les autres.* The heroine of the latter piece exults that
she was never anything more than a reflection of her
husband, that he could have made of her all the
women in the world, had his desires only been strong
and flexible enough. Simone de Beauvoir, going even
further, called woman's role-playing a noble means of
escaping an inferior destiny:

> The woman who finds pleasure in submitting
> to male caprices also admires the evident action
> of a sovereign free being in the tyranny practiced
> on her . . . it is intoxicating joy to feel herself the
> prey of another's free action.
> . . . one wearies of living always in the same
> skin, and blind obedience is the only chance for
> radical transformation known to a human being.
> Woman is thus slave, queen, flower, hind, stained-
> glass window, wanton, servant, courtesan, nurse,
> companion, mother, sister, child, according to the
> fugitive dreams, the imperious commands, of her
> lover. She lends herself to these metamorphoses
> with ravishment as long as she does not realize
> that all the time her lips have retained the un-
> varying savor of submission.[12]

Jean Anouilh has done his share of toying with the
idea. In his earliest works the matter was easy to
dramatize, so long as it was the single viable character
who did the dreaming and a blurry background figure

12. Simone de Beauvoir, *The Second Sex,* ed. H. M. Parshley (New
York, Knopf, 1953), p. 652.

who was idealized. Marc could transform his fiancée into "the purest, most courageous, most upright person in the world" (*NPN*, p. 15), and that was all there was to it. But when the playwright finally turned his gaze away from the heroes and onto their partners, he reacted fiercely. The heroine of *Y'Avait un Prisonnier* tried to lure her restive husband with a succession of contrived personalities, and, miracle of the feminine heart, they were all sincere, she said. Unlike Simone de Beauvoir, Jean Anouilh would equate a protean woman with a pack of lies.[13]

It has traditionally been man's role to mold woman to his ideal, and woman's role to attempt to embody that ideal. That *grand sincère* André Gide, who was less of a traditionalist in his roles than he liked to have people believe, confronted the problem rather gracefully in *Les Faux-Monnayeurs* when he wrote: "Involuntarily, unconsciously, each member of the couple in love fashions himself according to the dictates of the other, each works to resemble that idol which he contemplates in the heart of the other. . . . A person who really loves renounces sincerity."[14] It was the British critic Anthony Curtis who quoted the above passage in an excellently turned discussion of *Eurydice*.[15] Had his article appeared several years later, it probably would have contained equally perceptive remarks on *Roméo et Jeannette* and *Colombe*. For these are the plays which define Anouilh's tragic vision of love.

13. Cf. Lucien's vicious outburst against woman's adaptability, insincerity, and instability, in *NPN*, pp. 313–14.

14. *Les Faux-Monnayeurs* (Paris, Gallimard, 1939), p. 78.

15. Anthony Curtis, *New Developments in the French Theatre* (London, 1948), pp. 36 ff.

Eurydice is one of Anouilh's richest plays. It lends itself to a wealth of interpretations. For some spectators it is a work of utter despair, an unfortunate product of the war years. It is a eulogy to Death, they say, to beautiful Death, man's only salvation from the degradation of life. The *locus classicus* for this view is Orphée's outcry to Eurydice "I love you too much to live" (*PN,* p. 468). The altered myth can also be interpreted as an exposé of the power of the past, for the past brings guilt to the one and horror and vulnerability to the other. Or it may be said that it is the world (i.e. *other* people) which dooms Anouilh's lovers: Dulac slaps his image of a slovenly fornicatrix over Orphée's vision of a pristine madonna. And Dulac is not alone: a Pirandellian trial ensues during which each member of the cast thrusts his personal version of Eurydice before the befuddled lover. Certain spectators have remarked that while the classical Orpheus looks at—and thereby destroys—Eurydice out of love, a love so strong it can brook no conditions, Anouilh's Orphée gazes at his Eurydice out of jealousy: he wheels about to read the truth in her eyes as she would deny having been Dulac's mistress. Or they believe that the hero willingly destroys his beloved in order to prevent their still perfect union from ever being soiled by life.[16]

Now the work may be all these things, but it may also be a critique of the Pygmalion legend. Eurydice tries to embody the illusory woman with whom Orphée has fallen in love, and she fails. Early in the play, after

16. For a thorough and extremely provocative discussion of Anouilh's handling of the legend, see Eva Kushner, *Le Mythe d'Orphée dans la littérature française contemporaine* (Paris, Nizet, 1961), pp. 245 ff.

regretting her stupidity and her skinny body, she naïvely promises to become whatever her lover desires: one day she will be modest, another sensual, another mysterious or maternal or profligate or frugal or what have you. Her proposal is touching in its earnestness, but in retrospect it becomes poignant; for it is precisely because she has been unable to embody Orphée's desires that Eurydice runs away and is killed. You saw me as so beautiful (she writes him just before her death), so strong and pure—I never could have made it. Finally, as Orphée leads her up from death, he turns to look upon her—partly out of jealousy, it is true, but also in an effort to fathom this creature whom he may have created. Eurydice warns him in their climactic exchange, "Oh, please, my darling, don't turn around, don't look at me . . . What good will it do? Let me live. . . . Maybe I'm not the woman you wanted me to be. The woman you invented in the happiness of that first day" (ibid., p. 467). Orphée does not heed the warning and turns, and may we not say that his illusion fades at the sight of Eurydice? And has not Anouilh implied that Orphée's love was built upon dreams, that he had fallen in love with an idealized Eurydice, a Eurydice whom the heroine was quick to sense and willing to play? That such a love is possible only in fleeting dreamlike interludes, in the blind joy of first encounters, or in death should surprise no one.

The second text, *Roméo et Jeannette,* offers a slight variation. A couple quickly fall in love. The man refuses at first to recognize the baser traits of the woman, and she, in turn, attempts to mold herself according to his vision of her. No longer, though, does Anouilh resort to fantasy to reconstruct the complex character of his heroine; no longer does he let her flatly declare

her inability to play a part. Rather, he dramatizes
these elements. Unfortunately, the dramatizing is too
thin to be effective. Frédéric's sudden passion for Jeannette, we may recall, is not very credible: even before
he sets eyes on this tarnished angel, he knows all about
her. Thus limned from the outset in ugly lines, Jeannette, unlike Eurydice, cannot ingratiate herself in
our hearts without evoking mildly disturbing images
from her past. As a consequence, it is hard to believe
in her reformation, in her freshly bared inner purity,
in her new "role." This believing, of course, is the one
thing she asks of Frédéric; it is the one thing he obviously must have done as he fell in love with her; but
it is the one thing he no longer can do. Instead, the
hero turns inquisitor and destroys the personality—
or, should we say, the illusion?—that he himself has
just created.

It is not until *Colombe* that the theme finds worthy
expression and a remarkable technical solution. Once
again a woman is idealized by her partner and en-
couraged to play a role of his prescription. The couple
is shown in all the various moments of its predicament.
In the first act, as the conscripted Julien entrusts
Colombe to the care of his actress-mother, it is already
evident that he has forced his wife into an unnatural
position. Continue being the way I want you to be, he
begs her, and she replies that this is just what she has
always tried to do. But she clearly is not happy. She
huffs in Célimène fashion that she wants to be loved
like a real woman, not like a schoolgirl reciting les-
sons. Suddenly Julien reveals the magnitude of his
strange coercion by saying, *"gravely, slightly ridiculous:* If you love me, Colombe, you won't love anything that you love" (*PB*, p. 189). As the first act closes,

the heroine is already beginning to cast off her spurious role. Technically, only her hairdo has changed;
but as she and her husband gaze at her image in the
dressing-room mirror—he, uneasy and silent, she,
murmuring ecstatically, "It's me!"—everyone knows
that much more is at stake.

The second act traces Colombe's corruption at the
collective hands of the theatre people, especially those
of Julien's half-brother. The third act features her
denial of infidelity. It is a skillful rendition marred
only by a luxuriance of detail. Julien, just as blind to
the sullied dove as he had been to the pure, is now
ready to forgive his wife her "single" lapse. He even
admits having been too churlish in his efforts to make
of her the woman he wanted. But it is too late. Colombe blurts out the truth: she had never been happy
with Julien, she had always sacrificed herself to *his*
tastes, to *his* misanthropy, and now, she exults in one
of Anouilh's most overpowering and sustained scenes,
at last she is happy, at last she can be herself: the woman he loved, the woman he had tried to make her become, was a figment of his imagination. It was never
she. "Keep your lollipop Colombe, your little walking
virgin, if that's what you want. But I assure you, you
dreamed her up like the rest, my poor lamb" (*PB*,
p. 316). Left alone, Julien now recalls their first meeting in a dramatized epilogue. On this same bare stage
Colombe, the flower girl, had been offered a part in
one of Poète-Chéri's plays, but she had chosen instead
to run off with Julien. Julien (and the spectator)
wonders if the sweet and innocent Colombe ever really
existed or if he had not idealized her from the start,
forcing the nineteen-year-old girl into a role from
which one day she would escape.

Colombe's identity is the crux of the play, as Edward
Owen Marsh points out in his rich discussion. The
epilogue, he writes, "is an overwhelming climax, not
just an appended flashback. Dramatically it brings bewilderment to the highest pitch of intensity and under-
lines all the conflicting truths about Colombe which
Julien will never understand. . . . Which was the real
Colombe? And if the second is real, was the first not
so?"[17] According to Robert Nelson,[18] both Colombes
are real: she was and is a spontaneous, innocent ("not
hurtful") dove. Both Colombes probably *are* real,
though less from innocence than from fickleness; for
Anouilh, like Pirandello, has occasionally attacked
woman's instability and contrasted it to man's need
for permanence and form. As for the heroine's name,
we suppose it relates to her central weakness: facility.
Upon abandoning his wife, Julien warns her, "You're
so very little, and facility has such terrible traps . . . Be
afraid of facility with all your might, my little bird"
(*PB,* p. 188). A few minutes later he says gruffly, "Your
only faults are those of a bird, Colombe," to which
one might add, yes, she is flighty, and regret that La
Fontaine never saw fit to write the fable of facility and
rigor, of the dove and the bear.[19]

Anouilh appears to be saying in these plays that it
is folly to idealize our loved ones. Significantly, in
each of his romances he chose to dramatize the first
encounter between the lovers. And, we wonder, is it
the exigencies of the medium and simple tradition

17. Marsh, *Jean Anouilh,* p. 162.
18. *Play within a Play,* p. 152.
19. Nor did Anouilh, for that matter. His 1962 collection of *Fables*
was brought out in a limited book-club edition, and is unfortunately
not yet commercially available.

that have made the birth of love instantaneous in every
play? Or is it the fact that these people don't really
fall in love with each other, but rather with their
pre-existing ideals? Leonard Pronko, endorsing the
words of *Ardèle's* Count (*PG,* p. 59), puts it this way:
"Love, then, is but the projection of an ideal self into
another person, and when we say that we love another,
it is really our idealized self that we mean . . . each
loves himself in another."[20] Both Pronko and the
Count go too far, for a man's ideal need not be a version of his own self. Some people may ultimately be
in love with themselves. But there are those, including
many of Anouilh's characters, who idealize qualities
which are *not* their own. No, the unreal object with
which an Anouilh character falls in love is not necessarily a projection of himself; more likely it is what
psychoanalysts call an "imago": the idealization of a
loved one carried over from childhood into adult life.

20. *Anouilh,* p. 96.

6.   The Tragic Role

Anouilh's approach to tragedy is essentially a theatrical one. For him the stage is set for tragedy when an individual feels himself rooted to a role, irrevocably trapped in a part. What role? what part? The hero himself is not sure. All he knows is that it is *his* role, and as he plays out this still imperfectly illumined part, the tragedy unfolds. The climax is the epiphany; it is the moment of revelation when the hero finally discovers not his guilt or *hubris* but his very identity, the meaning of his role. And what is this meaning? Invariably, the role reduces itself to a lust for purity, to a thirst for perfection and principle —in a word, to idealism. Tragic circumstances have given the hero a choice: either he may compromise his ideals or else play out this demanding part to the end, to his death. In such a scheme destiny is no longer reflected in the flow and combination of external events; outside circumstances are in fact irrelevant, and all the impressive talk of well-oiled machines and rat traps to the contrary, the only fate weighing upon Anouilh's heroes is that of their own predestined idealism. This is why tragedy itself becomes for the playwright little more than a matter of *distribution,* of casting.

By building his tragedies around the disclosure of a hero's pre-established mission, Anouilh appears to have set himself apart from his contemporaries. True, Giraudoux once advocated in *Electre* the "declaring" of oneself, by which term he meant the acceptation and playing out of one's inner destiny. But there the notion was only incidental, and in later works Giraudoux abandoned it altogether. In fact, both in essays and subsequent drama (*La Guerre de Troie,* in particular) he went on to insist that an *external* destiny was vital to tragedy. He once even defined tragedy as man's perception of this superior force leading him about as by a leash.[1] As for existentialist drama, it would seem that Anouilh's tragedy lies at the furthermost pole from it; for what possibility do Anouilh's heroes have freely to decide what they are or to form themselves through their acts? Even Leonard Pronko, after noting several parallels between Anouilh's and existentialist theatre, admitted that in Anouilh the notion of roles was inherently deterministic. He could describe the freedom enjoyed by the playwright's tragic heroes only as illusory or, at best, confused.[2]

Anouilh's tragedies are often called metaphysical, because they treat man's unacceptable place in the universe. But could they not with equal logic be classified as tragedies of character? The emphasis is placed not on the idealism per se but on the gradual revelation of this idealism to the hero. Conflict anchors itself within each protagonist: having placed his values beyond himself, the hero is impelled at once toward life and toward the ideal; he seeks to reconcile the necessary with the impossible. It would seem that the success or failure of such tragedy should depend to a large extent on the impact of the hero on the specta-

1. "Bellac et la tragédie," *Littérature* (Paris, 1941), p. 297.
2. Pronko, *Anouilh,* pp. 60–75.

tors. Thus the playwright's principal task should be the fullest possible development of his tragic hero. Nevertheless, it is for this very character development that Anouilh has frequently been censured. Hubert Gignoux, Anouilh's most discerning critic during the Liberation, complained that the personalities of these heroes were more important to him than their tragic destinies: psychological drama stifles the tragedy, he said. At a performance of *Antigone* he was "a spectator not at the eternal conflict between order and truth, but at the conflict between a man and a woman 'who were not made to get along together.' "[3] We wonder whether Gignoux would have accepted Anouilh's characterizations more readily had he approached *Antigone* not so much as a struggle between truth and order but as the tragedy of a girl who comes to realize that she aspires to a purity which denies life itself.

Gignoux has raised other, equally typical objections. Discussing the optimum æsthetic distance for tragedy ("further away from the hero we would not pity him enough, but closer to him, we would judge him too much"), he finds himself so near to Antigone that he is conscious even of her physical person. The question of æsthetic or psychic distance is always a fascinating one—and its answer always subjective. One may or may not feel too involved with Antigone, too conscious of her body and brain, to appreciate her tragedy. Anouilh himself, it must be noted, was quite sensitive to problems of distance, especially in this play. At the very beginning the Prologue informs us that the heroine can already feel herself withdrawing at a vertiginous speed from her family and from us

3. Gignoux, *Anouilh,* p. 114.

all—though merely saying so does not make it a fact. The guards, who as caricatures are exaggerated far beyond the Sophoclean models, impart a loftier stamp to the protagonists by contrasting so boldly with them. As a matter of fact, the entire production was conceived with an eye to ennobling and dignifying the proceedings.[4] Certainly, had he so wished, Anouilh could have further increased the æsthetic distance by making his heroine less real psychologically. But his concept of tragedy demanded that we spectators truly believe in Antigone, that we fully accept her soul as it is revealed even to herself, and that we not dismiss her newly found thirst for purity as mere baggage tacked on to a rebellious girl solely to give her tragic stature.

Anouilh's concept of tragedy involves two dramaturgical problems. The first is how to make the fatality of a role so convincing that spectators will not reject it as arbitrary. The second is how, while operating within this closed universe, to make the revelation of a role exciting not only in its suddenness but in its context of grandeur and mortal struggle. Basically, the author's problem has been to reconcile predestination with dramatic disclosure: How can the hero be trapped in his part and not know what that part is? It is a tricky problem and one that Anouilh has attempted to resolve through a number of expedients.

Just which plays are the tragedies? None is so designated in the collected works, though *Antigone* was originally so labeled. Besides *Antigone,* we should include *Médée, L'Alouette, Becket,* and the fragment *Oreste.* Immediately obvious is a recourse to figures

4. See below, p. 161.

from myth and history, figures whose fates are readily acceptable as foredoomed.

Although it was not published until 1945, *Oreste* is generally held to be anterior to *Antigone*. The author has trapped the characters of his first tragedy in a Sartre-like hell: already cognizant of the outcome and significance of their acts, they are doomed to replay their lives forever. As everything has already happened, characters and spectators alike freely accept the roles as inevitable. But by the same token, the characters are so firmly rooted in their present condition that they are unable to break away and relive their pasts. Consequently, the slightest dramatic disclosure is inconceivable: Oreste cannot, in the heat of confrontation, suddenly discover that he will kill (or has just killed) Egisthe not out of revenge but out of desire for purity. The fragment is a dead end.

In *L'Alouette* the characters are again beyond their lives in some vague, stagy afterworld, represented by an equally vague and theatrical setting. As the curtain rises on a cast gathering up properties left behind from an earlier performance, the spectator immediately understands that he is witnessing a re-enactment; the tragedy is inescapable. Unlike the cast of *Oreste,* these people are effective actors: they have the capacity to escape their present condition and to lose themselves in scenes from their past. Thus they actually relive for the audience that dramatically charged moment of revelation. The dramatist's technical knowhow had evidently blossomed in the intervening years, for the utter freedom of treatment here and the graceful interplay of time and mood are overpowering. Simple narration, lighting changes, strong situations, dreams—anything may suddenly lift the spectator from one world and plunge him into another, more fanciful or more real, more joyous or more rending. The very ambiguity of time is turned to advantage. Early in the play it is implied that *L'Alouette* is taking place just after Jeanne's abjuration, while she is still in prison in Rouen. The object is to present the heroine's rise and fall as inevitable, and to approach the climax —that is, her retraction and her martyrdom—as part of the immediate, dramatic present. But even this present is far from a naturalistic one. Numerous interpolations and contradictions have already set the play in some fairy-tale world beyond reality, where theatricalism and ambiguity compound to render the lark's fate inevitable.[5]

If the climax of *L'Alouette* has any weaknesses, they are less of form than of content: Anouilh did not find a very ennobling motif for Jeanne's retraction. He fitted the scene into the standard mold of a protagonist suddenly discovering the meaning of his role, but he did so on a disappointingly homey level. After she has abjured, Jeanne is visited in her cell by Warwick, and the two begin musing about her future. Jeanne is depressed at the picture of herself growing old, fat, and complacent. She realizes now—but in retrospect, thus not very forcefully—that her true self is the maiden warrior. To recapture this true self and to hold it for-

5. For example, Cauchon: "In the course of this trial"; Cauchon: "We're not at the trial"; Jeanne: "You're confusing everything. At the beginning when I hear my Voices or at the end of the trial . . . when I abjured and then took it back"; Warwick: "Evidently, in reality it didn't happen quite like that"; etc. (*PC*, pp. 16–17, 20, 23, 82). The air of fatality is furthered by an occasional direct reminder, for example: "There's nothing we can do . . . We can only play our parts, each of us his own, good or bad, the way they're written, and in our turn" (ibid., p. 30).

ever, she retracts her confession and invites death.
Certainly, Anouilh's Jeanne d'Arc is a refreshing
figure; but her revelation is less glorious than ingenious. The dramatist found no better motive for his
lark's firmness of principle than a feminine fear of
aging.

In *Médée* Anouilh approached tragedy realistically.
No theatrical tricks make the action inevitable; it
simply unfolds on the evening of the heroine's death.
Yet the unrelieved, feverish pitch of the dialogue, its
poetic density, the series of protracted monologues,
the heavy utterances of foreboding—all impart an air
of doom and black necessity to the piece. As Médée and
Jason come face to face for their climactic encounter,
the latter declares that he cannot prevent Médée from
being herself; he understands that the die is cast. All
he can do is speak his heart for once. Indeed, they
both do, and their accusations and counteraccusations
constitute little more than an admitted domestic quarrel until, unexpectedly, each lapses into some fright-
fully deep self-analysis. Jason's disclosures are the
more significant, if only in their divergence from the
fundamental attitude of Anouilh's previous main
characters. But the grandiose reasons he suddenly reveals for having left Médée seem forced and out of
place: "I want to accept now," he says. "I want to learn
humility. This world, this chaos where you used to
lead me by the hand, I now want it to take on a form"
(*NPN,* p. 392). In short, he wants to be happy. Médée's
own revelation is just as contrived. From the beginning she has been characterized—even by herself—
solely in terms of her hatred and her vices. Now, at
the close of the play, even as she becomes the apothe-
osis of cruelty by committing the legendary murders,

suddenly she reveals a new facet of her personality: Médée is another of Anouilh's champions of purity. In her stylized death recitative she claims that she, too, was made for innocence and joy, that she, too, is principled and pure within. "I wish, oh how I wish, even this very second, just as strongly as when I was little, that everything could be goodness and light" (ibid., p. 400). But this eleventh-hour assimilation of Medean hatred and revolt into the search for purity is too contrived and sudden to impress.

In his latest tragedy, *Becket*, Anouilh has given dramatic form to the notion of inevitability by presenting the action as a simple flashback.[6] This flashback, however, is not developed with consistency: as the story is supposedly unfolding in Henry's mind, the play should contain only scenes which he himself has witnessed or learned about; but it does not. Obviously, point of view was not Anouilh's concern. What he was after was a feeling of finality, and once he had caught it, in the opening scene, he allowed his tragedy to evolve impersonally and naturally. Becket's discovery of his role could thus be immediate and dramatic.

Nevertheless, there are a few technical weaknesses in this tragedy. Becket's fundamental æstheticism (doing anything, but doing it beautifully) and his own awareness of this trait are bared early in the play. Hence his decision, upon being named archbishop, to be a good one, to defend to the utmost the Church (or

6. The device also allowed him to frame the story in irony: at the end, when Henry cynically dispatches Becket's known slayer to apprehend the murderers, it is obvious that political opportunism, and not conviction, has led the King to revere his late Archbishop.

the honor of God, as he calls it), is no less obvious or
predictable than his final decision to return to Canterbury. As Germaine Brée has pointed out, honor for
Anouilh's tragic heroes means little more than "fidel-
ity to the role one is designated to play, the acceptance
of oneself in a given part whatever its essential absurdity."[7] Once Becket has accepted his particular
role, the problems with which he wrestles (such as
whether to wear hair shirt or miter) are seldom earth-
shattering. What is worse, they are not even resolved
dramatically: instead of progressing through a series
of clashes with his antagonists, he arrives at his ulti-
mate understanding by reflection and recited prayer.
Indeed, Becket's story lacks dramatic intensity.

Perhaps it is in *Antigone* that Anouilh has most
successfully met the dramaturgical problems raised by
his concept of tragedy. Here, once again, the action
is irrevocably enclosed in a theatrical frame: a pro-
logue-character introduces the spectators to the members of the cast about to replay their tragedy. There
is nothing anyone can do, he says in formulas which
by now have become household words; they must all
play their parts to the end. Once the prologue has
settled the matter of predestination, the lights are
lowered, the stage cleared, and the story allowed to
unfold realistically. And yet a feeling of fatality pervades the entire performance. It is maintained both
by means of intermittent self-conscious lines (e.g.
"Each has his role. He has to put us to death, and we
have to bury our brother. That's the way the parts
were given" *NPN,* p. 144) and by means of a forceful

---

7. Germaine Brée, "The Innocent Amusements of Jean Anouilh,"
Horizon (Nov. 1960), p. 137.

intrusion of the chorus later in the play.[8] Whereas the
chorus and the audience may understand the fatality,
the characters do not: Hémon has no idea what is hap-
pening, Créon is convinced he can save Antigone, and
the heroine herself is (at first) interested only in bury-
ing her brother. But as the play builds to a climax—
and here Anouilh's genius reaches full sway—heroine
and spectator alike uncover the true meaning of her
role. Her destiny is not, as everyone has believed all
along, to subordinate civil obligations to those of
family or religion. Créon lets slip a few words in praise
of everyday happiness and all is over: Antigone
pounces on these words, and in a flurry of rhetoric she
suddenly understands that her role is to reject compromise, to spurn all life which is less than perfection.

What more may be said about Antigone's illumination? To begin with, it is a highly dramatic turnabout,
because it comes on the heels of her virtual acquies-
cence to Créon. Secondly, it is plausible, because it has
arisen not from a lovers' quarrel, as did the revelations
in *Médée,* but from an altercation pitting earthly order against divine duty. And finally, it is psychologically convincing, because it follows an intense and ex-
hausting argument, in which (reminiscent of Passeur's
or Raynal's theatre of violence) the very heat of argument has led to self-revelation. This was intentional:
Anouilh had his chorus introduce the key scene between Antigone and Créon with these words: "there is
nothing left but to shout—not moan, no, nor complain
—but to howl, at the top of your lungs, the things

8. This intrusion creates the necessary time lapse during which
the heroine may rebury her brother; and, indirectly, it has enabled
the author to present his touching, "free" Antigone, loving life but
calmly courting death.

you've always wanted to say and never have and which perhaps you never even knew before now. And for nothing: just to say them to yourself, just to learn them, yourself" (ibid., p. 166).

Concerning Créon's role, it may be noted that, while the first audiences in 1944 reviled him as a collaborationist, many have since come to regard him, and not Antigone, as the true hero of this tragedy of character. The prologue informs us that Créon has already felt ashamed of his base "official" acts, that he has adopted as a modus vivendi a blind and mechanical performance of duty. Hence, throughout the climactic scene both he and Antigone admit that, somehow, it is he who is in the wrong. Toward the end of their grueling encounter, Créon seems to awaken to the value of life itself, no matter how imperfect. But it is not until his shattering clash with Hémon that, pushed to the limit, forced to defend his actions before the accusing eyes of his son, Créon finally realizes that accepting life does not mean complacency in the face of all its horrors as one clutches at meager happiness; he realizes that to accept life is to accept being a man, to shed the comforts of infantile dreams, and to behold for once the world in all its beauty *and* ugliness.

Antigone is the tragedy of a girl who aspires to a purity beyond life itself. Life is unacceptable for her, and purity unattainable. The heroine, precast into a part which demanded death, is able to transfigure her role to tragic proportions by dying for this purity. The hero—for thus we may call Créon—equally aspires to the ideal, but finds himself thrust into the role of king, weighed down not only by his own life but by the lives of his subjects as well. He, too, plays his part tragically, by embracing the unacceptable.

7.   Scenic Vision

We have seen Anouilh's creatures reveling in the drama of their line-by-line life-performances. Now we see them turning inward, toward their pasts and their futures, to memories and dreams, on the trail of still more drama. They find it in a number of little scenes, which they may never play out on the stage but which they narrate with enviable facility, terseness, and piquancy of detail. Anouilh's characters have visions: they actually think in precise and vivid frames, frames that flash through their minds with cinematographic speed, frames that, when recounted, add a new dimension to the staged actions. Why do their minds work precisely in this fashion? Perhaps because the playwright himself is compelled to transpose everything—conflicts, ideas, characters, emotions—into palpable scenes. Or perhaps because Jean Anouilh is so obsessed with the theatre that he has projected this mental activity directly into his personages.

Scenic vision operates very simply. In *L'Alouette* Jeanne's father generalizes that sweet little girls turn into lying hussies, only he puts it this way: "A girl! She's as pure as a baby. She holds up her forehead for a goodnight kiss, and her eyes are so clear you can read to the bottom of her soul, one last time. And then, bang! The next morning—even though you locked her in—you don't know what's happened—you can't read a thing in her eyes any more, they flee you, and she lies to you! She's become the devil" (*PC*, p. 17). In *Roméo et Jeannette* Frédéric does not simply tell Jeannette that he can be happy without her. He swears that some day he will laugh: tomorrow, in a year, in ten years, Julia's and his child will make a funny sound as he learns to talk; the little dog they will have bought to amuse the children will become frightened of his own shadow; and so forth. In *L'Hermine* Monime offers herself to Frantz with a stageworthy dream of her defloration: "I want you to hurt me and make me bleed, I want you to smile and to sing afterward" (*PN*, p. 57). Thérèse, the *sauvage*, wants to overwhelm Florent with the degradations of her past life. "You were never ugly, or ashamed, or poor," she says in lines which may be found in any play (ibid., p. 208). But, significantly, she goes on to depict this past: cringing with fright in the stair well after having dropped a bottle of wine on an errand; taking detours to avoid walking down steps because of the holes in the knees of her stockings; the pregnancy when she was only fourteen; her delivery all alone in her room, dragging herself about on her hands and knees, bleeding, biting everything she could find to keep from crying.

Anouilh is by no means the first dramatist to have had characters recount nonstaged adventures. In modern plays of tight structure and heavy exposition, as well as in classical plays fettered by rules of time, place, and propriety, narrations of some sort have generally been unavoidable. Anouilh's are distinctive only in their theatricality. A glance at his expositions will bear this out.

If there exists any orthodox procedure for furnish-

ing expositions in modern plays, it is not that of brief-
ing servants, of explaining things to newly arrived
friends, or even of plunging directly into the action
and letting the situation gradually reveal itself. Rather, the single criterion is clarity, and the universal
practice that of stating the necessary background facts
in the most precise, graspable, matter-of-fact, and, unfortunately, uninspiring manner possible. The traditional exposition is something like a pesky medicine
the audience swallows grudgingly but greedily, a cure
for its preliminary ignorance.

This is precisely the sort of exposition Anouilh
offered in his first work, *L'Hermine*. The play opens
as Mr. Bentz refuses to aid the protagonist, Frantz, in
a hopelessly sinking business venture. It is vital to the
story to know exactly why Frantz sought great wealth
in the first place and what its deprivation will mean
to him now. To elicit this information, Anouilh, in
the opening moments of the play, directs Mr. Bentz
to raise point blank thirty-four questions and to drop
about half as many feelers. More important, he allows
the answers to these questions to be given in the
driest, most factual manner possible. And when Bentz
soon leaves the stage, Frantz's friend Philippe continues the questioning and allows the hero to unveil
his more secret motives. Insofar as *L'Hermine* is a
police drama, the swiftness and flatness of these inter-
rogations may be justifiable. The fact remains, however, that the exposition is very unimaginative and
heavy-handed; the spectator is continuously aware that
it is only a means to an end.

One exception in this early text sheds light on the
path Anouilh was to follow. As Mr. Bentz rakes over
Frantz's relations with the Duchess, Monime says, "My

aunt is very unkind to Frantz. When he's at the château, not a day goes by that she doesn't annoy him
some way or other." Dry, colorless, traditional. But
Philippe says, "They hit it off fantastically. The Duchess keeps staring at [Frantz] from behind her lorgnette.
Frantz keeps knitting his brows. Sometimes they speak,
but they never answer one another" (*PN*, p. 23). These
comments, somewhat better than Monime's, describe
the situation at the château. They have the further
advantages of being entertaining and requiring little
concentration on the part of the spectator, for an
image so deftly and wittily drawn is absorbed without
effort. In his subsequent plays Anouilh supplies the
exposition more and more by means of these sharp,
revelatory vignettes. It is as if he had discovered that
just as the whole dramatized work is an effort to communicate through a chain of highly selective scenes,
so, too, can the background material reduce itself to
scenes, equally selective, equally theatrical.

The playwright's growth in handling expository
material may be seen from the following two passages.
The amnesic hero of *Le Voyageur sans bagage* is appalled to learn that Jacques, his former "self," was
having an affair with Valentine, his brother's wife.
Valentine explains that it was always he, Jacques,
whom she had loved, he with whom she had played
tennis and gone swimming, he with whom she had ex-
changed kisses during their childhood summer vaca-
tions; and if she had married the older brother instead,
it was only because Jacques was too young, because
she was an orphan and the charity and patience of her
relatives were thinning. "Was I to sell myself to another rather than to him who would bring me closer

to you?" (*PN,* p. 322). Twelve years later, in *Ardèle,*
Nicolas returns to Nathalie, his older brother's wife,
whom he remembers having loved as an adolescent
and who once loved him in return. They meet secretly
under the stairs, as they often had in the past: "You're
here!" gasps Nicolas. "It's still two years ago. You've
come to spend your vacation at the château, as you do
every summer. We have until October to be happy.
I'll be grown up one day, I'll be grown up, you'll see"
(*PG,* p. 71). Rather than simply recall past events as
Valentine had done, Nicolas literally relives them
under the power of his emotions. Such manipulation
is superior, not only because Nicolas' violent emotions
are snatched up by the spectator, not merely because
a direct presentation is more powerful than an in-
direct one, but because the spectator is confronted
with two irreconcilable scenes: a tender one in which
he, together with the characters, would believe, and
an ugly one from which neither he nor they can escape.
The dialogue continues, as Nathalie explains why she
accepted the elder brother's proposal:

> I had refused all the others. You were still a boy,
> a prisoner in your boarding school, and my aunt
> had had her fill of supporting me. Her daily nag-
> ging, her eternal budgets . . . My shabby gloves,
> my coats so niggardly turned, my meager portions
> at table—I payed for them with my humiliating
> slavery for as long as I could. I read to her from
> all her devotional books, I got up at night for her
> bedpans and her medicines, badly dressed, under-
> fed—and grateful, of course!—for as long as I
> could.   [Ibid., p. 73]

The second version may be more developed, but the dramatist has not gained strength through length. He has found it by transporting us into the past, both through the imaginations of his characters and through their vivid speech.

The exposition of just about any Anouilh play consists of a series of sharply recalled scenes. In *Ardèle* the mainspring of the plot—the hunchback aunt's passion for a hunchback tutor—is communicated through shots of the two lovers seated hump to hump at the piano singing Fauré, or of their prancing through the prairie armed with butterfly nets. The exposition of *Médée* treats the death of passion: the dramatist had to establish that his whining heroine had long since ceased to love Jason. He could have been satisfied simply to have the nurse chide her, "You don't love him any more, Médée. You haven't desired him for a long time." But the ever incisive Anouilh continued and branded the image: "A person gets to know everything, cramped in this wagon. He made the first move one evening when he told you he was too warm and that he was going to sleep outside. You let him, and as you lay down that evening, I heard you sigh with relief to have the bed all to yourself" (*NPN*, p. 371).

Jumping ahead to 1956, we see the technique in its perfection. Outwardly, the exposition of *Pauvre Bitos* is accomplished through a hackneyed device: Maxime explains to a new arrival, Philippe, the circumstances about which the action will be built. Since Philippe is utterly unfamiliar with the situation, he asks only the briefest, broadest questions, and permits his host, Maxime, to talk at length. As the curtain rises, Maxime is showing Philippe the set, a huge hall he has just inherited. To the query, what does he expect to do with it, Maxime replies:

> Sell it. I sign next week with Shell. Yes, a garage. Ultra modern. All in neon. With pumps glowing like idols. They're going to splash concrete all over the place. That will teach my ancestors to have let themselves be guillotined like sheep. I abhor those stories of aristocrats mounting the scaffold, smiling with disdain. If only they had all barricaded themselves in here and died defending themselves like men, I would have held on to the building. [*PG*, pp. 375–76]

Maxime's ensuing lines will be equally pungent, and their imagery will be equally concrete. He has arranged a *dîner de têtes* (a costume party in which the head alone is disguised) for Bitos. "Bitos?" says Philippe. And Maxime answers: "Back at boarding school. That sneaky little scholarship student who was always first. (*He recites*) Latin composition, first prize: Bitos. Greek translation, first prize: Bitos. Mathematics, first prize: Bitos. It was the big end-of-the-year joke. We'd anticipate the results and scream them out in a chorus to the despair of the poor fathers" (ibid., p. 377). Rather than have Maxime state the facts simply and clearly, Anouilh cleverly transports us to the moment of the distribution of prizes. To Philippe's next question, what has become of Bitos, Maxime replies that, having been named deputy attorney general, Bitos has returned to town, and on a market day besides, wearing gray woolen gloves and toting a little clergyman's satchel stuffed with principles. The exposition continues as Philippe asks several more tradi-

tional questions and Maxime answers, always with one
or two well-chosen, devastating images. By the time
Bitos arrives on stage ten minutes later, nothing will
have happened,[1] but the spectator will have a perfect
understanding of theme, plot, and characters. What is
even more important, he will have been continuously
diverted by a barrage of background anecdotes.

It must be evident by now that these narrations have
more than an expository value. They are really metaphors, visual metaphors, and as such they make palpable any abstraction. No longer is the spectator asked
to think *about* poverty, rigor, or waning love; instead,
he is allowed to experience them directly, to feel their
weight. Just as Rousseau knew that the only way to
describe an emotion is to show its effects, Anouilh
seems to know that the only way to communicate to a
theatre audience emotions (and notions) is to set them
in context: the spectator now lives them just as he does
in reality.

Narrated scenes may also be valuable as characterizing devices. While everything a man says or does,
down to his minutest gestures and peculiarities of
speech and dress, reveals something of his personality,
in the long run—and this is especially so on the stage
—actions are more revelatory than words. Unfortunately, the amount and kinds of stageable actions are
limited. Anouilh would seem to have hit upon the
admirable expedient of placing his creatures in a series
of intense and highly revelatory incidents that are not

1. As a matter of fact, not too much happens during the entire
three acts, which is conceivably one of the play's weaknesses, and
which may account for Anouilh's strenuous efforts to theatricalize
his matter through the brittle, stagy dialogues of Maxime and his
friends.

enacted but reported. He establishes character by, and he transposes character into, nuggets of pure theatre.

What could tell us more about André Bitos than his own actions in this macabre little scenario, and how, one wonders, could the feelings of the narrator toward Bitos better be depicted, all before Bitos has even set foot on stage?

> Bitos had won the death penalty for a minor collaborator some time after the Liberation. Actually, this fellow was an old schoolmate of his and the two had maintained their friendship right until the war. This happened three years ago. Oversight, red tape, delays, hesitations, who knows? The fact remains that for three years our humanitarian regime kept the fellow in the death cell, in leg-irons, waiting for every dawn. Last week they up and remember him and, for no reason, apparently, decide that they'll execute him after all. The poor wretch's wife makes an appeal, weeping, accompanied by her little girl. Bitos, more and more the virtuous Roman, suffers with her—and sincerely, I'm sure—but he doesn't yield. [Ibid., p. 385]

The description continues, with piercing detail piled on piercing detail: the actual execution, when Bitos permits the victim to cry "Vive la France!" and "Fire!"; Bitos' reaction ("He takes out his watch and says matter of factly, 'We have respected the timetable.' A station master!"); and his final gesture in giving the little girl a doll ("to replace her daddy, no doubt. A very expensive doll, too. That's what's beautiful: Bitos is poor. More than half a month's pay. A doll that closed its eyes, said papa and mama and made water. As a matter of fact, it was a German doll, for, even if the government was still executing people, business was quite alive again"). No matter how sensational the incident may be, it takes a certain nerve to include in a contemporary play a narration of such length. Yet the vigor of Anouilh's style, his corrosive wit, and the sheer theatre of the recounted episodes keep a twentieth-century audience listening—and seeing.

Indeed, characters are etched with surprising swiftness and economy through such narrations. In *La Valse des toréadors,* which is a farce, the personnages are caricatures notwithstanding the authenticity of their emotions. The story concerns a husband who delays consummating an idealized love affair for seventeen years out of respect for an invalid wife who, for her own part, has for seventeen years never ceased despising and betraying him—just the sort of scrape any poor devil is liable to run into. Now Anouilh could conceivably have treated the incidents straightforwardly, enlisting our sympathy for these sad creatures, especially for the near-mistress, innocent, passive Ghislaine de Sainte-Euverte, victim of the General's cowardice and of his wife's deceit. To ensure against this, the playwright had Ghislaine instantaneously register across the footlights as a ridiculous old spinster. To these ends he placed her in two of the most banal situations of the old-maid repertory. Only he recounted them, he did not dramatize them. With her first panting breaths on stage, Ghislaine tells the story of her voyage—the night train, the sinister man in her compartment, the ordeal, the defense: "Had he moved a hair, had he but touched the hem of my dress,

I would have shot him, and then myself. I had to be pure when I reached you, Léon" (*PG,* p. 104). Getting her second wind, Ghislaine now re-enacts the extravaganza of her first meeting with the General seventeen years earlier: they sing, they waltz, he ogles, she swoons. And Ghislaine, as the sexually menaced old maid and again as the simpering romanticist, is twice caught in the perfect tableau. Recalled scenes have advanced the characterization and exposition in an essentially theatrical manner.

Conflict in *La Répétition* stems from the Count's betrayal of his wife. He betrays her not by recruiting a new mistress but by falling in love with a nursemaid: the intended liaison augurs public humiliation for the Countess. Anouilh's first task (rendered more difficult by the intricate plot and by the fact that the drama begins at an advanced moment) is to impress the audience with the strict code of his aristocrats, not merely a code of exclusiveness and elegance, but one which by its studied egotism precludes real love. Otherwise the very heart of the play may be lost—the infamy of the Count's behavior, his wife's mortification and hatred, and, above all, the magnitude of the Count's emotions, toppling all his previous values, virtually recreating him as a fresh, beautiful child, introducing him to a world that, from fear of ridicule, his class has graciously spurned. To accomplish this, Anouilh might have unleashed his cast of characters and simply let them directly impose their acrid standards upon us by their accumulated actions and reactions. This, however, would have taken time, and much of the early drama might have been lost. The author's solution was to communicate the aristocratic code swiftly and vividly by means of a series of recounted vignettes.

The opening speeches of *La Répétition* may appear excessively talky on the printed page, but in truth, they are merely a succession of theatrical scenes—scenes which, taken together, perfectly convey the peculiar attitudes of this strange cast.[2]

Narrated scenes have any number of applications. Sometimes they advance the plot. In *L'Invitation au château*, for example, Horace anticipates a stunning speech he is about to deliver to his guests, and several moments later the spectators are able to follow other actions concurrent to, and influenced by, this speech. Also, narrated scenes may be exploited for humor. As we have seen, Anouilh is never above larding his dialogues with anecdotes, especially during the opening moments. Like the gags the destitute writer peddled in his youth, such anecdotes have no other purpose than to arouse laughter, and they succeed, with the help of their vivid imagery. In *La Valse des toréadors* a general dictates a passage from his memoirs and pauses to reminisce on the plight of two missionaries, captured and returned as cadavers, tied together like sausages, their testicles between their teeth. Early in *Colombe* Madame Georges compulsively traces her family medical history and muses over her tubercular child, the gentle one, forever spitting in his little corner or playing alone with bits of wood. Actually, these anecdotes are not always as gratuitous as they may appear: they sometimes embody Jean Anouilh's "ideas."

According to the handbook, a playwright with an

2. A similar eruption of exterior scenes early in *Antigone* acquainted the spectator with the heroine's biography and made her ensuing tragedy more moving.

idea is not supposed to tell us about it; he is supposed
to demonstrate it, to incorporate it in a story whose
emotional and intellectual impact will communicate
it to us directly. Not only we but the protagonist as
well can be made to understand without having it
spelled out that *hubris* doesn't pay—or even, as we
may glean from a Montherlant work, that it does pay.
Obviously Jean Anouilh does not follow the book. He
has spent thirty years, it would seem, rewriting the
same play around the conflict between purity and
compromise, and has nevertheless gone on to sermon-
ize in each of them on purity and compromise. But
is there anything inherently wrong with such discours-
ing? The best way for anyone to communicate an idea
forcefully is to concretize that idea, whether it be in
parables, proofs, or precedents. And if an entire play
can be construed as a living parable or illustration of
some thesis, why can't the writer further theatricalize
his play by including within it still more illustrations
of that thesis? One reason, with respect to Jean
Anouilh, is that his stagemanship outpaces his intellect. No matter how he has varied his approaches, no
matter how vividly he has probed the eddies and
backwaters of his thought, the central dilemma of
every play has invariably reduced itself to "How can
social man gratify his principles without in some way
or other losing his pants?" Still, the number and variety
of illustrations he has devised to embellish this theme
are not only prodigious, they are always highly theatrical as well, and glazed with pungent, provocative
detail.

The man who for years during the Fourth Republic
lived almost within earshot of the Chamber of Dep-

uties has seen fit on several occasions to advance the
following argument:

> But someone has to take command of the ship.
> It's full of crime, misery, and stupidity, it's taking
> on water from all sides. . . . The crew won't do a
> thing; they think of nothing but raiding the hold;
> and the officers are already busy making a com-
> fortable little raft, just for themselves, with the
> entire provision of drinking water. And the mast
> is splitting, and the wind is howling and the sails
> are about to rip.   [*NPN,* p. 184]

The brave and battered ship of state is a brave and
battered image; but Créon does present it here with
extreme vividness. Since the war, Anouilh's parables
and sustained metaphors have tended more toward
parody. Sometimes he has set them in frames of irony:
such would be Ornifle's panegyric of constant love to
his son's fiancée, whom he immediately undertakes to
seduce. More often, though, the speeches support
blatantly ignoble views. Typical are the General's
spicy and specious precepts in *La Valse,* reducing hon-
or to that old bugbear: appearances. In *L'Hurluberlu*
there is a multitude of didactic analogies: the General
sends a hundred roofers toppling to their graves to
destroy the myth of utilitarianism; his friend Lebelluc
compares women to cigars; the curate compares women
to panthers, and with such cynicism, it must be noted,
that quite a few of Anouilh's associates objected to the
lack of verisimilitude (treat her like a kitten, he says,
feed her shreds of raw meat and lumps of sugar, scratch
her back, let her frolic with you, but never forget that
she can suddenly smell blood, turn back into a panther,
and, still adoring you, strike you dead). A favorite im-

age of love (and ingratitude) is that of the pelican who feeds its offspring with its own viscera. Anouilh has returned to it again and again, though perhaps nowhere has he etched it more ferociously than in *Colombe:*

> The people who are dangerous in this world, the real troublemakers, are the ones who simply *must* give away their guts . . . They rip open their bellies, reach in, and spew their guts out over the world. It's disgusting! And the more it hurts, the more they love it. With racking pain they keep grabbing them by the handful, just to offer them to us, whether we want them or not. And we stumble, we suffocate in their guts . . . [*PB,* p. 320]

8.   Effects of the Vision

The inner visions of an Anouilh character are often so intense that they blind him to outer reality. One moment he may nurture a smoldering memory, another, a mere figment, but it is always imagination, and not actuality, that runs his life.

A theme which once so obsessed Anouilh that it became virtually synonymous with his theatre is that of memory. Armand Salacrou once suggested that human beings are more miserable in their misery than they are joyous in their joy. Those inclined to embrace Salacrou's law would no doubt happily go along with its corollary—that warmed-over misery is tastier than warmed-over joy. And Anouilh's characters would surely agree. For them a good memory is a bad memory; vivid, scenic recollections are a bane, not a boon. "Since I was a boy all my memories have been wounds," says Julien; "Behind each of us there's much too nasty a story," says Vulturne, speaking for all Frenchmen; "a morning will come, a brand new morning without memories," says Frédéric.[1] In play after play, at least during Anouilh's early period, the protagonist was possessed by his memory, pinioned under what we may call an apparitional guilt complex, so

1. *PB*, p. 192; *PG*, p. 418; *NPN*, p. 340.

beseiged by visions of past traumas that he was unable
to break away and assert his real (or potential) goodness. This was the dilemma of Marc, Thérèse, Gaston,
Georges, and Eurydice, and it comprises the central
theme of the works to which we now turn.

Marc has committed no wrongs, but he is the son
of Jézabel; he assumes her guilt and renounces happiness and marriage. To dramatize the sense of inherited
guilt, he evokes a number of scenes from his past,
scenes of his mother's infidelities and neglect. Poi-
gnantly, he longs to be an orphan, free of all memories.

Thérèse, the *sauvage,* bearing in addition to the
guilt of her parents that of her own past, also flees an
idealized fiancé. By ascribing her vices to the environment, however, Anouilh allows Thérèse to remain essentially pure after having behaved, in fact, most
wantonly. Even in Thérèse's own mind some ambiguity remains as to the depth and validity of her corruption. Guilt, then, can only partially explain her
flight. There is a humanitarian motive as well. By implying that humanity is the by-product of thwarted
desires, Anouilh shows the wealthy, talented, uncrossed
fiancé to be divinely inhuman; he is incapable of ever
touching Thérèse in her soul, that organ composed
entirely of scar tissue. Thus Thérèse bolts less from
guilt than from the conviction that she would be de-
serting humanity by attaching herself to such a man.
Her father, it has been pointed out,[2] is the dramatic
symbol of the heroine's past turpitudes. By his mere
presence on stage, he imposes these turpitudes on the
rest of the cast. Still, his presence does not stop Thérèse
from eagerly resurrecting more tableaux from her past,

2. Robert Champigny, "Theatre in a Mirror: Anouilh," *Yale
French Studies, 14* (1954–55), 57–64.

some of them quite sensational, and verbally flinging
them in the face of her fiancé—less in proof of depravity, we suppose, than in proof of her humanity.

The traveler without luggage is a man without a
past, and he is happy and kindly without one. Gaston
may indeed have dreamed from time to time about
his childhood, but these fancies were the very antithesis of the ugly facts the Renaud family now thrust
upon him. Conflict rages not so much between the
Renauds, who would impose, and Gaston, who would
deny, as within Gaston himself, where two opposed
beings confront one another, the one good, the other
evil. To this extent Gaston is an Everyman, and his
story is one of Anouilh's most absorbing and universal.
The play's success depends to a large extent on the
effectiveness of the images depicting these two contradictory souls. Scenes from the past thus form the
body of the play; they are numerous and they are justly vivid. Some early exchanges on the hero's former
toys set the tone for what is to follow. Handed a huge
slingshot with which he used to kill birds, Gaston recoils in horror. No, he cries, when he was seven he
used to go into the garden and feed the sparrows little
crumbs of bread from his hands. "The poor devils,
you would have twisted their necks," says the older
brother (*PN,* p. 294). The Renauds go on to enumer-
ate the various tortures he used to inflict on animals;
they brandish before him other toys—knives and
rifles—while Gaston can only vainly search for puppets and sailboats. Subsequent scenes from the past
are etched with equal starkness: they include pushing
his best friend down a flight of stairs, striking his
mother, sleeping with his brother's wife, and a few
other peccadillos.

Georges, the hero of *Le Rendez-vous de Senlis,* resembles Thérèse in that he has remained pure through a lifetime of depravation and would assert his essential goodness in a liaison with an innocent partner. Unlike Thérèse, however, he has lied about his past. In fact, he has created an ideal past to befit his idealized fiancée. As in the earlier play, the wicked past is dramatized by members of the family, who this time rush onto the stage quite to the hero's dismay. It is also evoked verbally to clarify a few of Georges' obliquities; but such scenes are flat beside the more forceful imprint made by his family.

Eurydice is heavy with past, and it was not begot by Orphée. Rather than unburden herself in Thérèse's flamboyant manner, she withholds and prevaricates. When she sees that the truth will out, dreading the weight of her sins on her lover, she flees. Recalled scenes are vital to this play, for the lovers are destroyed essentially by Eurydice's past. In the supernatural third act a number of incidents are re-enacted, but throughout the rest of the play they are narrated, often in Anouilh's most felicitous dialogues. Perhaps nowhere is the hallucinatory grip of memory better expressed in words than during the touching second act. For several moments the lovers do nothing but recall tableaux of their childhoods and of their day-long life together. Eurydice then asks if the ugly parts of one's past remain with one, as well. Yes, always, replies Orphée; and the heroine suffers to think that every hand that has touched her must remain forever glued to her skin. Before the vague promise of purification through confession, she hesitates: What if confessing doesn't work? What if the horrors of the past were to continue "twice as alive, twice as strong, for having been repeated; what if the other person were to remember them forever, too?" (*PN,* p. 424). Technically, such talk is superflous in *Eurydice,* as it would have been in any of the preceding plays, because Anouilh's heroes have all behaved as if they had felt exactly what Eurydice admits she feels: that a shameful past is a living past. But dramatically, these exchanges are sound. There is a certain warmth, pathos, and urgency to Eurydice's words; they flow from an inner necessity that raises them beyond mere expounding. Salacrou, who shares so many of Anouilh's themes, offers a telling comparison. In *Le Miroir* (1956) he attempted a similar explication, but it quickly degenerated into "pirandelirations":

> LUCIEN: . . . Our past does not die. Our past is our eternity. . . . you will understand when you're old that a gesture doesn't fade away, it is perpetually reborn, and at twenty you're already old with your future old age, and at fifty you're still young with your past youth. We're condemned to be the person we were. Even if, later on, we believe that we didn't want to be the person that we were.
>
> CECILE: You're forgetting that God's pardon can efface all our sins.
>
> LUCIEN: No! No! Pardon is a fruit of sin, and sin lives in the heart of pardon.   [I.3]

One cannot overemphasize the significance in Anouilh's early works of the theme of guilt through memory. His theatre has been variously dubbed a "theatre of memory," "a drama of shame," and "a

desperate search for purity.''[3] The past in these plays
has been compared to romantic destiny, and love to
the purifying passion of the romantics. An Anouilh
character wavers between the pure world of nonbeing
and the corrupting world of life, causing the critics to
evoke Valéry's *La Jeune Parque*. He wishes to throw
off his past and become a new man, causing them to
cite Musset's *Rolla* or lines from Baudelaire. Not in-
significant have been the religious interpretations of
the theme. Since 1946, when Robert Kemp first referred specifically to the baptism motif in Anouilh's
theatre, it has become commonplace to remark that
his soiled and sinning heroes aspire to moral rebirth.
(One critic even went so far as to call baptism the unifying myth of Anouilh's theatre.)[4] Hubert Gignoux,
considering Thérèse's guilt to be impersonal and to
stem from the mere fact that she is born of the Tardes,
saw parallels in the accursed families of Greek tragedy
and, particularly, in the descendants of Adam and Eve.
According to Gignoux, Thérèse does not envisage that
she can be reborn in innocence until she has seen
Florent weeping: "She is amazed, she suddenly understands that man can be redeemed by suffering."[5] And
Gignoux only adumbrated what the more conscien-
tious Catholic critics, like Maxime Chastaing, have
since formulized in terms of sin, saviour, crucifixion,
and redemption.[6]

3. Robert Kemp, in *Erasme* (Oct. 1946), p. 400; Grossvogel, *The
Self-Conscious Stage*, p. 155; René-Marill Albérès, *La Révolte des
écrivains d'aujourd'hui* (Paris, 1949), p. 141.

4. Kemp, *La Vie du théâtre*, p. 95; Robert Brasillach, "Jean
Anouilh, ou le Mythe du baptême," *Les Quatre Jeudis* (Paris, 1951).

5. Gignoux, *Anouilh*, pp. 47–48.

6. Chastaing, "Jean Anouilh," *Esprit* (March 1947).

There have been others who have displayed less
enthusiasm for the message—holy or otherwise—of
Anouilh's early works. They have balked at his "ma-
donnas of the gutter," his "angels on the dunghill."[7]
And especially since Julia emerged uninfected from
the same environment that bred sister Jeannette, they
have openly mocked the ill-fated heroine who pines
for a ravished purity: "She dreams of purity—then
why did she not stay pure?" they ask.[8]

But the truly fascinating aspect of this once-obses-
sive theme is the author's own sudden disenchantment
with it after *Médée*. "These horrible contradictions,
these abysses, these wounds, I reply to them now by
the simplest gesture man ever invented to live: I reject them," says Jason, freeing himself from memories,
absurdity, rebellion, and Médée (*NPN,* p. 393). When
the frenetic woman defies him to forget her, Jason
replies that despite the bloody traces he *will* forget,
he *will* learn to live in peace and a semblance of order.
According to one's point of view, Jason may seem
something of a sophist after a bit of cheap happiness,
or again he may seem like the first of Anouilh's heroes
to have a grain of common sense. One thing is certain,
however: as Gabriel Marcel astutely observed, Jason's
farewell to Médée is Anouilh's own farewell to his
anterior work. Henceforth his protagonists will no
longer regard the sins of their past as irremediable or
even expiable. They will just forget about them. Both

7. See, for example, Harold Hobson, *The French Theatre of Today, an English View* (London, George G. Harrap, 1953); and Joseph
Chiari, *The Contemporary French Theatre: The Flight from Naturalism* (London, Rockliff, 1958).

8. Jacques Carat, "Anouilh romantique et giralducien," *Paru*
(Nov. 1947), p. 44.

the Count of *La Répétition* and the General of *L'Hurluberlu* manage to come upon a pure love after a substantial lifetime of licentiousness. Had Colombe been treated with more understanding by her bearish husband, one suspects she might have lived in bliss for all her premarital indelicacies. And Thomas à Becket, despite some perfunctory grumbling about the difficulty of shouldering the honor of God, does not seem, on his maiden voyage to sainthood, exactly overburdened by the baggage of a lecherous past. Had Anouilh himself acquired the wisdom of saints while he was obsessed with what we may cynically call their apprenticeship, would he ever have written of the indelible scars of youth? Or would he have concluded that blemishes, like beauty, are only skin deep?

Now if these early characters' memories were mainly of humiliation and guilt, they were also, to a small but significant degree, of beauty and innocence: these people idealized their childhood, and implied that the tragedy of man is to have outgrown that childhood. Some critics, perhaps exaggerating the importance of a handful of lines in these early texts, have defined young Anouilh's central theme as a regressive longing for the purity of childhood.[9] They have invariably pointed to Gaston's cry of triumph as he refuses his past, "I am a man and I can be as new as a child"; to Orphée's sigh to Eurydice, "One day you'd have to breathe me with your breath, you'd have to swallow me. It would be wonderful. I'd be so small in you; I'd be warm and happy"; or to Antigone's myriad references to her childhood, especially her final exclamation, "I want to be sure of everything today and I

9. See, for example, Francis Ambrière, in *Les Annales* (Sept. 1956); and Chiari, *Contemporary French Theatre.*

want everything to be as beautiful as when I was little
—or I want to die."[10] Evidently, such an interpretation is not without grounds. But neither is it a master
key to young Anouilh's thought. Particularly as regards *Antigone,* it is hard to know whether the heroine's evocations of childhood scenes are only a trick to
render moving an essentially abstract argument, or
whether, indeed, she just does not want to grow up
and her tantrum-like quest for death is the embarrassing conclusion of the playwright's infantilism.
Perhaps all one can safely say is that the evocation of
past scenes is the most effective technique Anouilh
could have used, even if he were after all only wailing
the "Extra-Uterine Blues."

Just as these characters are plagued and swayed by
visions from the past, they are also dominated by visions from the future. Maeterlinck and Tristan Bernard used to claim that a theatre audience is affected
more by what is merely suggested than by what is
physically enacted on stage; and to the extent that an
audience is endowed with imagination, their theory
may be valid. Jean Anouilh's characters resemble such
a highly imaginative audience, in that before the spectacle of their own lives they are moved less by hap-
penings than by suggestions, less by outer realities
than by inner visions. Their imaginations are stronger
even than their senses or their reason (a distinction
Pascal would have them share with the rest of humanity). It may be argued, of course, that we are all
motivated in the long run by our cerebration, and in
novels it is an easy matter to communicate. But in
today's fast-paced theatre, without Shakespearean

10. *PN*, pp. 348, 465; *NPN*, p. 193.

monologues, without Racinean tirades, without end-
less Shavian discussions, without the metaphysical
digressions of Pirandello or Salacrou, how is one to
dramatize the workings of the mind? Most American
playwrights, it would seem, have given up the attempt
altogether. Anouilh may have offered a compromise of
sorts between the equally unsatisfactory theatre of
violence and the more stodgy theatre of ideas by
peopling his works not with men of thought but with
men of imagination. Throughout the plays—and
Anouilh has shown remarkable consistency here—it
is not violent actions which in turn precipitate violence and prod the characters on to peaks of emotion;
it is instead a mental image which motivates them:
the dream of a perfect love, a rankling memory, the
anticipation of a joy which will never be, the halluci-
nation of an unbearable horror. A climax may be
assiduously and logically prepared, but it is invariably
triggered by a precise vision in someone's mind.

In *L'Hermine* exactly what impels Frantz to murder
Monime's aunt? The playwright has already established the motive and the opportunity for the crime,
but now, to generate the emotional intensity that will
precipitate the act, he has Frantz gaze upon Monime,
this pure, idealized girl whom he himself has corrupted, and conjure up a series of images: Monime in
a white dress, Monime by the murmuring brook,
Monime with the smile of deceit, Monime under the
greasy hands of an abortionist, Monime climbing
trees, running across the lawn, etc. These violently
contrasting visions of his beloved overwhelm Frantz
and give him the impetus to execute his previously
obscure plans of murder. Similarly, Antigone finds
the courage to bury her brother by summoning up the

image of him returning triumphantly from a dance
and presenting her with a paper flower. Before stran-
gling her children, Médée works herself into a feverish
pitch by evoking the image of a rigorous and pure
little girl called Médée. Why does Jeanne d'Arc re-
tract her confession? Psychologically, because she may
not be keen about a lifetime in prison; philosophically,
to be true to her role; but dramatically, because she
has suddenly glimpsed Jeanne slipping into middle
age, accepting, compromising, gourmandizing, primp-
ing. And these prospects so repel her that she immediately chooses death. In *Le Rendez-vous de Senlis,* as
Barbara takes leave of Georges, who is now in the arms
of another mistress and awaiting possible imprison-
ment, she is moved to tears. And by what? By the memory of her first days with him, when the two adulterers
used to play cops and robbers.

For centuries dramatists have had their characters
imagine and anticipate precise scenes, inspired by
spiritual visions or, more pertinently, by that highly
cerebral emotion, jealousy. Othello, for example, was
lost long before he discovered the handkerchief. When
Iago recounted Cassio's dream ("Then he laid his leg
/ Over my thigh, and sighed, and kissed . . ."), Othello
was already so overcome by jealousy that the mere
thought of Cassio lying "with or on" Desdemona drove
him into an epileptic fit. In contemporary French
theatre Salacrou is noteworthy for his exploitation of
this technique: his jealous lovers are particularly gifted
in inflicting upon themselves visions of their partners'
infidelities—visions which, in turn, goad them to re-
newed jealousy. The classic example on the modern
French stage remains Jean-Jacque Bernard's *Le Feu*

qui reprend mal, the story of a French soldier, André, who returns to his wife in 1918 to discover that an American officer has been billeted in his home. He is immediately convinced of his wife's infidelity and leaps to a reconstruction of the scenes of betrayal:

> ANDRÉ: That's where *he* used to sit, too, isn't it?
> BLANCHE: Him! . . . Ah! be quiet . . .
> ANDRÉ: Didn't you used to tell *him* to be quiet, too, whenever he'd talk about me? (*Rising.*) Didn't you used to stand in this room exactly as we are now? And this table, it was always set for two, wasn't it? (*Looking about.*) Ah! his ghost will follow me everywhere. He's still here, watching, moving—he's alive inside you.
>
> [Act I]

Even the denouement is effected by equally cerebral means. Blanche, harried by her husband's insane jealousy, resolves to leave him, but when she pictures André living alone in those same surroundings, she stays.

All such visions are quite tame alongside the ravings of Anouilh's Amélie Saint-Pé, insane from jealousy in *Ardèle,* and supposedly crippled from jealousy in *La Valse des toréadors.* Her hallucinatory outburst in the former work is a barrage of sexual imagery, culminating in a partial listing of the objects of her husband's lust: the mother superior who presided at his sister's taking of the veil, Gilberte Swann, the wife of the President of the French Republic, etc. And in the following play Amélie's imaginative faculties seem to have developed, for she can now enter the lascivious thoughts of her husband. The piece opens with an interesting accusation:

> Where were you just now in that vile mind of yours? With what woman? . . . in which pantry polishing off God knows which maid? She was down on her hands and knees scrubbing the floor. You slinked over on your fat slippers like a fat old cat. You grabbed her from behind. You bite her neck, you have all her hair in your mouth and it doesn't disgust you, you who fly into a rage when you find just one in your soup! And she hasn't even removed her apron, that pig! In the odor of scrub water! On the floor, like animals! You make me sick, Léon!   [*PG,* p. 92]

Actually, the motif of jealousy is surprisingly rare in Anouilh's theatre; besides Amélie, only the lady cellist of *L'Orchestre* is particularly smitten by it. Rather, it is love that is manufactured through the infusion of imaginary scenes. By conjuring up fantasies from the past or future, Anouilh's lovers inspire themselves with passions that far surpass those induced by realities. In fact, at times one wonders if they have not abandoned altogether those old-fashioned, prosaic avenues of stimulation. As heroes, they are enamored of their own lost purity; as lovers, they are naturally attracted to their partners' former state of purity. Hence Orphée and Eurydice, within a few moments of their first encounter, imagine and recall one another's childhood; the vision of little Orphée carrying his violin case and trudging behind his father or facing arrest at a sidewalk café brings tears to the heroine's eyes. As for dreaming of the future, it has probably

always been a sacred right of lovers. Giraudoux, in
Amphitryon 38, wrote a delightful scene in which
Alcmène and Amphitryon idly dream about their
golden anniversary and even pretend they are living
in the softness of their autumn years. The scene might
have been quite moving were the protagonists not a
shade too self-conscious, conjuring up scenes, one
suspects, primarily to demonstrate their own and their
creator's dexterity. In Anouilh's works such pretending radiates with more spontaneity: the lovers appear
simply to let their feelings spill over into the future.
And, as always, their images are extremely precise;
they are more disturbing than reality itself.

Consider, for instance, the role of imagination in
three of Anouilh's love scenes. *Le Rendez-vous de
Senlis* hinges about a young man's desire to realize a
certain dream: Georges longs to spend a pleasant evening at home with his parents and with his sweet
fiancée, Isabelle. Regrettably, Georges' existence has
been so corrupted that to live his dream he must resort to playing it out with hired actors in a rented
house. The plan understandably goes awry, and Isabelle finds herself face to face with the naughty truth.
She asks Georges for only five minutes' explanation.
Georges responds with frankness and humility. He
reminisces over his own childhood, stenciling in a few
scenes from the typical Anouilh repertory: falling
asleep on the kitchen table while awaiting mamma's
return from an afternoon of dallying, papa's locking
himself in a room full of toy soldiers, and so forth.
He then, in contrast, imagines the many evenings Isabelle must have spent in her home, protected by generations of benevolent grandmothers. When Isabelle
understands that Georges really loves her, she says

that this knowledge is sufficient for her happiness. Now occurs one of the most touching moments of the play:

> GEORGES: You're right, let's be happy. (*He dreams a moment.*) How demanding people are! We begin by claiming nothing less than a lifetime of happiness; then we learn that a few stolen years are a rare piece of luck . . . Afterward we settle for a single evening . . . And then, all of a sudden, only five minutes are left, and we manage to find that even they are an infinite oasis, five minutes of happiness.
>
> [*PR,* p. 235]

The two lovers play out their entire lives together in these five minutes. Isabelle acts as if the game were but a prelude to the realization of their dreams, but Georges—and the audience, too—suspect that it is nothing more than a game, and that when the allotted time is over he must fall back into his habitual depravity. Nevertheless, *Le Rendez-vous de Senlis* is a "pièce rose," and as the final curtain rings down on yet another imagined scene, that of the ideal family dinner as originally conceived, the author begs our complicity in the affirmation of his hero's rebirth: Georges has been purified by Isabelle, and the two lovers will know happiness after all.[11]

In *La Répétition* imagination again engenders and elicits love. The Count has discovered the sentiment

---

11. Critics have generally had misgivings before this patently false ending. No one is duped, they say, for were there but another scene, this "pièce rose" would turn into a "pièce noire." In fact, *Le Rendez-vous de Senlis* is a perfect illustration of Schopenhauer's generalization that comedy must always drop the curtain swiftly at the moment of joy, so that no one may see what comes after.

most theatrically by portraying the enamored prince of the play within the play, *La Double Inconstance*. Lucile's feelings, too, may have been nurtured by her role in the Marivaux play, but her awareness of them grows from some fanciful chatter early in the second act. Declining the Count's roguish advances, Lucile counters with some fast talk of her own—about the man with whom one day she expects to fall in love and about the way he will approach her. The Count is astute enough to urge Lucile to speak on of this imagined love; she complies, her own words infecting her with the very emotions she is supposedly only describing. Under the spell of her dreams, under the charm of the highly romantic Marivaux play, and, of course, with some gentle guiding from the Count, Lucile now grazes the truth from a different but equally unreal angle: she evokes the Count's youth. She pictures him with cane, white gloves, and derby, on his first manly stroll down the proper boulevards of Paris. "I see you quite well. It's difficult, isn't it, to grow up?" As the Count feigns exasperation, she hurries on: "Don't get angry. It's rather nice to have remained a little boy" (*PB*, p. 382). Declarations of love are only breaths away. But the essential point here is that it has been imagined scenes, and not direct experience, which helped generate an emotion and have led to a display of that emotion.

A final illustration can be drawn from *Roméo et Jeannette*. The second act takes place during the evening of Frédéric's arrival at the home of his fiancée, Julia. He sits alone in the slowly darkening living room, with Julia's sister, Jeannette, and the audience quickly senses that he and Jeannette have fallen deeply in love. Anouilh once admitted that this second act ran away with him.[12] So, too, we would add, did his use of imaginary scenes; for the entire act, as it progresses to a declaration of love and to flight, is basically little more than the series of tableaux with which the two lovers impassion themselves and each other. Several seconds after the curtain has risen, Frédéric says he has the impression that he and Jeannette are somewhere in the distant future and that it is Julia they have returned to visit. He embroiders the picture for a moment, until Jeannette's objections force him to transfer his pretending into the distant past. And this is only the beginning: the rest of the act is every bit as fanciful. Indeed, the imaginative prowess of this couple is so acute that one would almost believe them destined to a lifetime of indecent bliss. Toward the end of the act, as the moment of declaration draws near, the dialogue gets particularly mawkish and confused. The two have been struggling all day long, says Frédéric, but without having touched each other, without having dared to look at each other; even now they are still far apart. "We mustn't, not even once, imagine ourselves in each other's arms," he warns. "We mustn't tomorrow," whispers Jeannette, with closed eyes, "but this evening I am in your arms" (*NPN*, p. 267). And now she summons up the "negative" vision of the bride she can never be, the bride in white, an image that has haunted Anouilh since his first plays. Still, underneath she is just as pure, she cries, and only for Frédéric if he deign see. And, to be sure, the vision sends him reeling across the stage and into her arms. Their doom is sealed.

All these lovers share a certain psychology. They

12. Kemp, *La Vie du théâtre*, p. 95.

apparently need to reduce the raw matter of experience into something more assimilable; they are compelled, as it were, to transpose reality into fantasy. Nor are they at all sensual; for even when they set to imagining scenes, they don't choose them from the immediate past of lingering sensations or from the near future of breathless anticipation. Instead, they lose themselves in faraway settings, in scenes of childhood or of old age. Giraudoux, for all his intellectuality, often had his lovers imagine or simply examine the physical presence of their partners, trait by trait. Anouilh's lovers, too, may dwell on one another's physical features, they may evoke a slender or fleshy body—but always to illustrate some moral quality. Never do they evoke a beautiful face, a smile, or a voice for the sheer joy of talking about what they love.[13]

Even serious talk about physical love—i.e. "I'll enter you and I'll believe for a moment that we are two intertwined stems of the same plant" (PN, p. 465)— is extremely rare; for Anouilh clearly regards it as a "gesture," and contemptuously dispatches it along with all the other gestures of men. In a shabby hotel room with Orphée, Eurydice reflects: "Everyone who has ever been here is all around us, the fat ones, the skinny ones, the monstrous ones, their bodies knotted

13. On the other hand, Anouilh's caricatures, his lechers rather than his lovers, do have a bent for noting physical details—and nothing else. Typical are Ornifle's remarks as he follows Fabrice's report of his past escapades: "ORNIFLE, *eating and drinking, delighted:* Tall, blond, stupid, admirable thighs. Did they put that in your report? . . . That's all there was worth remembering about her. Yes, quite so, I had taken the Orient Express with a pair of thighs. An admirable pair of thighs encumbered by a young blond woman with whom I never knew what to do in the afternoon" (PG, p. 321).

together. . . . The bed is full of them. Gestures are ugly" (ibid., p. 428). And the lovers are loath to repeat this particular gesture, to put themselves at its mercy, to allow their love to hang by the unsightly thread of animal coupling. Even General Saint-Pé declined consummating his liaison with Mlle. de Sainte-Euverte, because, in his words, he was "afraid of breaking the charm by repeating the same gestures with her" (*PG*, p. 138).

The fact is that for all his violence and theatricality, Anouilh has never written a searing love scene. The greatest amount of passion in his work is generated over malevolent vanity or rage. Just as there is no corporeality to his brand of love, so there is no passion or tension to it. Consistently, it is presented in its aspects of peace, calm, and tenderness—feelings which the characters always delight in seeing come so quickly. "As if one had arrived somewhere," says Julien to Colombe two minutes after they have met; "I never could bear anyone's touching me," says Lucile, "but when he took me in his arms, I felt that I had finally arrived somewhere . . . That's all"; "He really touched me! And suddenly I was no longer alone. . . . I put my foot ashore, at last," says Mlle. de Sainte-Euverte. And the General himself expresses this feeling in its extreme, almost malignant form: "It's that, suddenly, I was no longer afraid. . . . It was my soul, leaving me the hell alone."[14]

We do not know why Anouilh has been so reticent about dramatizing a more passionate love. It is remotely possible that he chose to limit his romantic passages to a few striking motifs (i.e. two little brothers,

14. *PB*, pp. 329, 447; *PG*, pp. 194, 137.

arriving) in order more clearly to impose these very personal views on his public. Or perhaps he simply considered it inelegant to dramatize passion, and, with his noted *sauvagerie,* has taken a graceful pirouette away from a delicate subject, one possibly requiring greater lyric gifts than he may possess. But it is just as likely that the artist's potent imagination has had some bearing on the matter:

> A hundred concordant details make one presume that he confused, in very good faith, the emotions of his imagination with the troubles of his senses, or, to be more precise, that his temperament, similar to Rousseau's, was commanded by imagined visions rather than by real contacts. Perhaps at birth he possessed a direct and real sensuality, but the first timidities, the first compromises deflected it and, so to speak, caused it to rise entirely to the brain. Hence love, as he describes it, is a cerebral state, corresponding to the extreme tension of imagination, not to the ultimate conclusion of desire. It is Platonic . . . with that Platonism . . . which is its own fulfillment and which confuses the dream of love with love.

This revelatory and apt reflection was made by Léon Blum about another equally cerebral romantic, Stendhal.[15]

15. Blum, *Stendhal et le beylisme* (Paris, Albin Michel, 1947), p. 154.

9.   Style

THE COUNT: . . . Naturalness and truth, in the theatre, are the least natural things in the world, my dear. Don't think it's enough to recover the tones of life. In the first place, the text in life is always so bad! We live in a world that has completely lost the practice of the semicolon; we all speak in unfinished sentences that fade into three little dots because we never find the right word. And then, the so-called natural conversation which actors claim to copy—that gasping and drooling and stammering and hesitating—really, it's not worth the trouble of assembling five or six hundred people in an auditorium and asking for their money just to give them a spectacle of that sort. They adore it, I know, they recognize themselves in it. Even so, one must write and play the comedy better than they do. Life is very pretty, but it has no form. Art has as an object precisely to give it form. [*PB*, p. 387]

Many aspects of a dramatist's style derive from the fundamental question posed and resolved in the above passage: Should the dialogue be an imitation of real speech or should it be the creation of superior speech? Since 1936 Anouilh has maintained

his particular views with consistency. It was then, he
tells us, that he first understood that the theatre's truth,
in language just as in character and situation, must
be founded not in life but in theatricality: "My real
shock in the theatre was Giraudoux. I've done nothing, I hope, that resembles his work. But it was Giraudoux who taught me that there could be in the theatre
a language that is poetic and artificial and yet truer
than stenographic conversation. I had no idea of this.
It was my revelation."[1]

So much for Anouilh's theory. It could not be
plainer: a dialogue should have beauty, poetry, and
artificiality. But what of the praxis? The Count's very
words, above, a model of linguistic grace and precision,
imply that the artist has, in fact, practiced what he
preaches. And a glance at some early dialogues, those
written before 1935, during Anouilh's naturalistic or
stenographic period, might further confirm our impression; for the beauty and poetry here were, at best,
life's own: "LA COPINE: . . . Ecoute, ma petite . . . Moi,
je vais te dire quelque chose. Les boniments, tu com-
prends, c'est bon. C'est utile, avec les hommes, on sait
ce que c'est. Mais quand on est honnête, si tu veux
que je te dise, on les fait pas à ses copains, les boniments."[2] ["THE PAL: . . . Listen, dearie . . . I want
to tell you something. You see, claptrap is fine. It's
handy with men—we know what they are. But when
you're on the level, if you don't mind my saying so,
you don't use that claptrap on your friends."] From
copine to count is a linguistic light-year. And yet,
despite the obvious elevation of language, despite the

1. *Les Nouvelles littéraires* (March 27, 1937).
2. Anouilh, *La Sauvage,* in *Les Oeuvres libres* (Paris, Fayard,
1938), No. 201, p. 22.

pretentious theorizing and the undeniable debt to Giraudoux, it is not really a *poetic* idiom that Anouilh has striven for through the years; it is a *dramatic* one, an idiom oriented less toward poetic beauty than toward the traditional dramatic values of clarity, concision, and rhythm, and toward the personal dramatic value of artificiality. It goes without saying that Anouilh has never attained the "completely" dramatic dialogue; neither could the symbolists ever create a poem containing nothing but poetry. Stylistic concepts are only relative, and to gauge Anouilh's relative success in the handling of language, to grasp his clarity, concision, rhythm, and artificiality, we shall perforce turn to a number of comparisons.

Because a dialogue must be grasped instantaneously —on the wing, as it were—the playwright's first task is to make himself easily understood; his primary concern is for clarity and its corollaries, simplicity and emphasis. Just about any passage from Anouilh's theatre could be exhibited as an end product of such concerns. But the instrumental art, the craftsman's maneuvers toward these goals, can best be felt when one studies his single adaptation of a nondramatic work, Louise de Vilmorin's *Madame de* . . . . As the novel is, to begin with, of a classical design, written with the utmost economy and reserve, and as Anouilh's adaptation (unfortunately still unpublished and unperformed in France) is little more than a stage reading of the Vilmorin text, the few minor changes that he has inserted take on greater relief. They are of two sorts, reduction and expansion, but their single goal is clarity. Entire phrases and, especially, qualifiers have been cut for the sake of simplicity, and Louise de Vilmorin's bare sentences have been further stripped

to make their meaning sharper and more emphatic.
When, on the other hand, the original lines were already too brief or too bare to carry across the stage
and register in the spectators' minds, the dramatist has
given them needed body. To make certain contrasts
and comparisons more distinct, Anouilh has inserted
conjunctions and repeated personal pronouns. Whereas Louise de Vilmorin could establish an intricate
situation on the assumption that the reader would re-
tain the particulars, the dramatist has had to be more
prudent, and when sufficient stage time has elapsed
for his audience to forget an essential point, to avoid
any possible ambiguity, he has reintroduced this point.

If Anouilh has striven for directness and transpar-
ency of languages in his plays, he certainly has not
been obsessed by these qualities in his other writings.
Possibly, it is only in these nondramatic writings that
the author's "natural" or authentic style is to be seen.
The following typical period from his "Lettre à une
jeune fille qui veut faire du théâtre" is perfectly logical
in its development; it is incisive, limpid, even vivid
in its imagery; but in an auditorium it would exhaust
and confound everyone. In fact, a few moments of
language like this would constitute burlesque:

> Car c'est de cela qu'il est question, en fin de
> compte, dans votre lettre et dans votre vocation.
> De "couper" à la vie, au choix de vous-même; à
> l'obligation pour votre âme de trouver l'unité en
> elle, de dégager son authenticité des méandres de
> nos velléités, de nos faux désirs, de nos mirages
> (nous en avons, nous aussi, vous savez!) de la
> mettre à nu, au lieu de la déguiser d'oripeaux
> tous les soirs et—après tout, vous êtes une jeune

fille—quand vous aurez trouvé le garçon, le vrai,
que vous aimerez et que vous lui tendrez vos
lèvres, que ce ne soient pas des lèvres qui aient
déjà dit: "Je t'aime" à un autre jeune homme
peinturluré la veille, et qui, le soir même de ce
don de vous (car les comédiens n'ont que les
après-midi pour aimer à leur compte) rediront
encore "je t'aime" à un autre jeune homme
peinturlé sous les regards de cinq ou six cents
personnes—et peut-être de la même façon.[3]

[For ultimately, in your letter and in your voca-
tion, it is a question of "escaping" life on your
own terms, of escaping the obligations of your
soul to find its inner unity, to draw its authenticity from the labyrinth of our velleities, our false
desires, and our mirages (we also have them, you
know!), to strip it bare instead of disguising it
with tinsel every evening, and—after all, you're
a girl—when you find the boy, the real one, whom
you will love and to whom you'll offer your lips,
may they not be lips which have already said, "I
love you," to another young man smeared with
paint, the night before, and which, the very evening of this gift of yourself (for actors have only
afternoons to love on their own), will again say
"I love you" to another young man smeared with
paint, under the eyes of five or six hundred people
—and perhaps in the same way.]

It was probably this same quest for stage clarity that
misguided Anouilh into overdoing his scenic directions. Certainly, painful experiences may have taught

3. *Elle* (Jan. 21, 1955).

him that the playwright can never be too explicit if he
would prevent future misinterpretations of his texts.
And yet, isn't one of the theatre's greatest resources its
very adaptability to varying reinterpretations by the
performing artists? At any rate, it is amusing to note
that the man who has admired French classicists for
their mysteries and abysses, for the very fact that they
do not spell out their thoughts as ineptly as do our
contemporary Freud-smitten artists, is the same man
who in his own works has inserted a truly staggering
number of stage directions—staggering not only in
their sheer bulk but in their explicitness, nuance, and
superfluity. (For example: "with the shadow of a smile
on his thin lips"; "his tone is imperceptibly false";
"CHARLES, *asks:* Is he dead?"[4] In fact, scanning the
directions of Anouilh's texts, one sometimes has the
feeling that the plays are pantomimes and not dramas.[5]

Such directions do, of course, facilitate our reading
of Anouilh's plays, especially insofar as we are un-
trained laymen, incapable of or unaccustomed to
imagining the various stage business and modes of delivery. To the professional, such unabating precision,
while annoying, obtrusive, or even insulting, is not
really an obstacle; for if performers look upon the
printed dialogue as sacred and, by tradition, never
tamper with it, they rarely consider scenic directions

4. *PG*, pp. 426, 463, 475.
5. Once, in a volume of adaptations, Anouilh imposed some
heavy clarifying on texts which in their native language seemed to
have nicely weathered any inherent ambiguities. Whereas most of
the staging addenda are quite judicious, a few would inevitably
irritate even the most broad-minded Anglo-Saxon reader of his *Trois
Comédies de Shakespeare:* e.g. "Leontes thumps him nicely on the
head"; "Enter Le Beau, an affected and ridiculous old gentleman"
(*Trois Comédies de Shakespeare,* pp. 135, 15).

as much more than guide lines. Little is lost, therefore, while clarity and nuance are definitely achieved.

The second traditional quality of good dramatic writing is concision. Anouilh's characters do not waste words. This may seem a rash statement in the light of the Paris production of *Becket,* which ran for almost four hours (despite several deletions from the printed text) or that the author managed to prune a good thirty minutes from *Ornifle* several weeks after the opening. The concision in question is quite unrelated to the over-all composition of the works. It refers rather to the word-by-word arrangement, to the stylistic discipline and tightness which Anouilh has perfected in the course of his career. Those inelegant ellipsis dots so abhorred by the Count in *La Répétition,* those stumbling phrases and that bungling syntax which everyone finds himself improvising, each in his own slipshod way, those almost compulsive repetitions, those false connective crutches, those flat expletives, those clumsy fillers—in short, the redundancies, tautologies, and protractions once commended by Zola for the naturalist theatre—do they not form the matrix of that early play, *Y'Avait un Prisonnier?*

> MARCELLIN: . . . tu n'aurais pas dû me dire ça. Non, là! tu n'aurais pas dû me dire ça.
> LUDOVIC, *le regarde; un silence:* Non, je n'aurais pas dû te dire ça. Mais, d'ailleurs, écoute, Marcellin . . .
>   . . .
> MARCELLIN: Mais, vous croyez, je ne sais pas si je dois . . .
> BARRICAULT: Si, si. D'ailleurs, il vous a appelé.

MONSIEUR PEINE: . . . Et . . . bonne chance.

MARCELLIN: . . . Oui, mais enfin . . . il y a si long-
temps, et puis, en somme, l'autre, le bagnard,
je ne le connais pas du tout . . .

[MARCELLIN: . . . you shouldn't have said that to
me. Uh-uh, no! you shouldn't have said that to
me.

LUDOVIC, *looks at him; a pause:* No, I shouldn't
have said that to you. But, anyway, listen,
Marcellin . . .

. . .

MARCELLIN: But—you think so? I don't know if
I should . . .

BARRICAULT: Yes, yes. Anyhow, he called you.

MONSIEUR PEINE: . . . And . . . good luck.

MARCELLIN: . . . Yes, but just the same . . . it's
been so long, and then, when you come down
to it, the other one, the convict, I don't know
him at all . . .]   [*YA,* pp. 24, 19]

Were Anouilh to revise the play today, were he simply
to include it in his published works, there is little
doubt but that the above passages would be severely
cut. The author's present-day style, his shorn, sharp,
and classic handling of language, is not so readily
demonstrable as the naturalistic manner, but a few
of its qualities may still be cited: rarely now does a
character fail to communicate his precise thoughts;
rarely does his phrase trail off in an abortive series of
dots; rarely does a speaker contradict or interrupt himself without having finished his thought; never will
his interlocutor interrupt him before the thought is
achieved. Repetitions and echoes are reserved either

for emphasis or for mimicry and moments of utter confusion.[6]

The third standard attribute of dramatic writing is rhythm. It is generally held that the rhythm should vary from moment to moment and person to person, and that not simply rhythm but style itself in drama should be, ideally, a multiplicity of styles, each of which is readily assignable to a particular member of the cast. In his early, naturalist years Anouilh was not yet expert enough as a craftsman to have set his speech in disparate patterns, to have charged his dialogues with hurtling rhythms. For example, Tarde, as grotesque as he may be, does not speak any differently than Florent France or, for that matter, than Thérèse herself. Soon, though, as the playwright gained mastery of his medium, as he followed Giraudoux's path away from naturalism, he developed an electric and diversified style, one in which each character might find his own rhythm and his own key.

L'Hurluberlu is the play of rhythm par excellence. Not only is there a continual oscillation between pink and black in the course of the four acts, but each character has his own language, intonation, body movements, and gestures, which combine in a distinctive, unique pattern. The General's coarse and vinegary speech crackles with virility and precision. His wife talks in a soft, musical lilt, at once crystal-pure and crystal-sharp—"inexorable," the playwright specifies. The speech of the conspirators is equally personal and

6. E.g. "DAVID EDWARD MENDIGALES: . . . You, for example, General, you're the perfect example of the man who doesn't know how to live. THE GENERAL *murmurs, as if fascinated by David Edward Mendigalès and his logic:* I'm the perfect example of the man who doesn't know how to live?" (*HU*, p. 173).

equally distant from the eschewed stenographic language of naturalism. Tinpot Ledadu jerks and clowns through a series of distilled barbarisms. The flaccid Lebelluc mumbles and shrugs his way into a state of utter physical and moral depletion. Belaxor, under cover of a farcical refrain and falsetto, displays his peculiar blend of articulateness and depravity. And Mendigalès, bandying about the latest pearls from Introductory Psychology and Beginning Bohemianism, is the verbal embodiment of youthful insolence and cynicism.

Besides aiming at traditional clarity, concision, and rhythm, Anouilh's style also contributes to the over-all artificiality of the plays. Now had the dramatist worked in verse or in an incantatory prose, his success or failure on this score might have been more easily evaluated. But he forged a style that is neither to the left nor to the right, neither naturalistic nor poetic; he has written neither from the stomach nor to the cortex; and it is not always easy to show just where and how language has furthered that broad transposition of reality into theatricality which forms the heart of his æsthetic. All the observer can do is to put his finger on a few stylistic peculiarities or variants that seem to accentuate this theatricality.

Through the years, Anouilh's dialogues have grown increasingly urbane and elegant. Although the casts of characters have been growing urbane and elegant, too, there has apparently been no search for linguistic verisimilitude: nursemaids, soubrettes, and flower girls speak just as felicitously as counts and popes. Any number of characters employ language quite incongrous with their station in life—and in plays like these it doesn't matter. Immediately there comes to mind the pot merchant Ledadu's own use of the word "incongruous" just an instant after having been nonplussed by scarcely more learned words. (Even Anouilh's associates in *L'Hurluberlu* were unable to deter him from this purported blunder.) Moving toward refinement and elegance of language, the playwright has understandably attenuated, though not eliminated, coarseness in his dialogues. It should be noted that his present attitude is one of mild indulgence: "In the country of Molière and Rabelais, ears are not as delicate as the press has recently claimed," he wrote in the wake of *La Valse des toréadors*.[7] Refinement, like most good things for bad people, is worth talking about only in the breach, and if it was breached in a few lines of *La Valse*, it was trampled underfoot throughout most of *La Grotte*. But then, *La Grotte* is an "unwritten" play: its action has not yet been transposed into theatricality (so claims the actor-author) and its vulgarities may therefore be forgiven. What is more, a central theme of *La Grotte* is the impassible gulf between the worlds of aristocrat and servant; hence differences of speech between these two worlds are appropriate.

Passing on, one notes that the anachronisms which abound in the historical and mythological plays also give the texts an air of artificiality. A few, like the machine guns of *Antigone*, are visual, but the majority are verbal, and when they are uttered in moments of grandeur (often within clusters of familiar language), they pique and disconcert the spectator, and, whether he likes it or not, heighten his feeling of participation in the work. As for the epigrams which Anouilh now

7. *Figaro* (Jan. 23, 1952).

scatters through his comedies, while they are not designed to increase theatricality, they obviously do so.
Here are five of them, and they are typically uneven:
"Women always feel pity in the face of wounds they
themselves have not inflicted"; "Sincerity is an artifice
like any other"; "A man is rich when he has nothing
to lose"; "Love is the bread of the poor"; "Intelligence
. . . is the weapon of the poor."[8]

There exist, as of now, only a few variants to
Anouilh's texts, but their direction is clearly toward
increased theatricality and artificiality through language. *L'Hermine* (1931) and *La Sauvage* (1934) were
both printed in *Les Oeuvres libres* (1934 and 1938,
respectively), before undergoing minor revisions and
appearing in their definitive form as "pièces noires"
(1942). Although variants may be cited that point to
increased clarity, concision, and concern for rhythm,
the general movement is away from naturalism (colloquialisms, solecisms, and slang are recast into correct
French; vulgar expressions are discarded; a youthful
tendency toward sensationalism is somewhat curbed),
and toward a more polished, subtle, artificial idiom.
Here is one pale illustration: "Oh! là là . . . la vieille?
J'espère qu'elle te laissera beaucoup d'argent, car elle
t'aura beaucoup embêtée . . ." becomes "Comment?
Pas encore morte, cette vieille dame? Elle manque
vraiment d'esprit d'à propos. Dites-lui de se dépêcher,
que c'est beaucoup trop long!" (*PN*, p. 63). ["Oh my,
the old woman? I hope she leaves you a lot of money,
for she's caused you a lot of trouble." . . . "What? Not
dead yet, that old girl? Really, she has no sense of tim-
ing. Do tell her to hurry, she's been much too long!"]

8. *PG*, p. 421; *PC*, p. 255; *PB*, pp. 402, 364, 427.

Ironically, when *La Sauvage* first opened, it was the "sincere" vulgarities that the critics most admired, whereas they were rebuffed by the so-called oratory. A number of revivals, one generation, and a bare version later, yesterday's oratory has blossomed into today's poetry; and Anouilh's sordid world, while unavoidably receding from present realities, has lost none of its truth.

Even though he has perceptibly elevated his language, Anouilh has never shied away from syntactical liberties that might bring vigor and clarity to the dialogues. This is an important point, and one which American audiences may not fully appreciate. Too many of the English adaptations of Anouilh's plays have tended to emphasize his elegance and urbanity at the expense of his power. Anouilh's style is purposefully uneven and jarring; it is at once elegant *and* vulgar, at once titillating *and* abrasive. If he has composed dialogues of grace and crackling precision, he has also made them fairly bristle with colloquialisms and unliterary syntax. There is no English equivalent to the French, "Et pourtant, j'en ai de la rigueur, tous mes amis vous le diront . . ." spoken by the Author in *La Grotte* (p. 36), or to Lucien's "Vous pouvez la danser jusqu'au bout la danse maintenant" (*NPN*, p. 314). The more stylistically correct forms would be less effective in the auditorium. In short, with Jean Anouilh, as with all true dramatists, problems of style reduce themselves to problems of rhetoric.

As for pastiches, the playwright has openly imitated other authors on two occasions. In *La Répétition* he not only recreated the characters and intrigue of Marivaux's *La Double Inconstance* but also succeeded in duplicating the elusive style—so well, in fact, that as Anouilh's characters rehearse scenes from Marivaux's play, it is difficult to know where one text leaves off and the other begins. To critics *La Répétition* was a virtuoso piece; and if they marveled at the alliance of stories, they marveled even more at the fusion of styles. For the deceptively simple dialogues of Marivaux have invited and defied mere analysis, let alone imitation, for over two centuries. Traditionally, *marivaudage* has been called a "métaphysique de l'amour," and been explained quite vaguely as elegant, precious flirting. Recently, however, the French scholar Frédéric Deloffre has offered a more convincing definition of the idiom: it is "a voyage to the world of truth," he has said, a movement from linguistic ambiguity (the conscious or unconscious dodging of one's sentiments) to linguistic clarity (the declaration of one's love, often simultaneous with one's first consciousness of it).[9] The delicate scene-weaving between Lucile and the Count, examined in the previous chapter, was marivaudage steeped in exactly this sort of linguistic ambiguity; for underneath the pretending, the couple was making love. And true to Deloffre's formula, once their love was openly declared, at the end of the second act, *La Répétition* abruptly veered away from Marivaux's universe and drifted toward the brittle and black ambiguities of Anouilh's own game of pretending.

Inserted in *L'Hurluberlu* is a spanking parody of the French avant-garde theatre, *Zim! boum! ou Julien l'apostat, antidrame*. On a barren stage garnished by a lone *bidet* (whose significance is "profoundly metaphysical"), *Zim! boum!* brilliantly exposes the absurdity and nothingness of the human condition. Ironically, it also pokes fun at some traits found in Anouilh's

9. Frédéric Deloffre, *Marivaux et le marivaudage* (Paris, Les Belles Lettres, 1955), p. 8; cf. pp. 207 ff.

own writing. The abuse of anguished silences and the pseudocomic prolongation of certain stage business bring to mind, in particular, a droll ballet in *Pauvre Bitos,* directed to last "to the limit of the spectators' resistance" *(PG,* p. 423). Now whether Popopieff, author of *Zim! boum!,* represents Ionesco, Adamov, or Beckett is open to speculation; but his identity is of less significance than the fact that it was Anouilh himself who, just a short time earlier, had measurably launched Ionesco on the road to fame and fortune with a front-page article in *Le Figaro* of April 23, 1956. After calling *Waiting for Godot* "one of the three or four masterpieces of contemporary theatre"—praise he had already sung when that play opened[10]—Anouilh indicated that Ionesco's *Les Chaises,* currently struggling for survival at the Studio des Champs-Elysées, was superior, that it was "black à la Molière." A scant two years later, in *L'Hurluberlu* (completed in 1958, but not produced until 1959 to avoid any misinterpretations involving another general who was also conspiring at the time), he was turning the whole movement to ridicule. That very recently he was back in *Le Figaro,*[11] again expounding on the final absurdity of the human condition, makes one wonder how much conviction went into *Zim! boum!* and how much plain zest for caricaturing. Stendhal once chafed and raged before his countrymen: nation of vaudeville players, he dubbed them, a race ever eager to joke for the mere sake of appearing witty, but utterly unconcerned about sincerity. Anouilh the bear, Anouilh the man of rigor and principle, may be better adapted to his habitat.

10. *Arts* (Feb. 27, 1953).
11. Oct. 1, 1962.

10.　Staging

If theatricality is the unifying principle behind Anouilh's handling of plot, character, and language, it is even more assuredly the key to the staging
of his plays. Once again, the artist's concern is not so
much to represent the world *in* the theatre as to present the world *of* theatre; once again, his goal is not
to *translate* reality but to *transpose* it.

The big red curtain opens, and even before the
spectators can lose themselves in the story, a host of
lies, distortions, and artifices impress them with the
theatricality of what is to follow. The curtain itself
may even play a role. Occasionally, a secondary gauze
drop-curtain will turn the stage into a picture book.
In the early months of World War II, Anouilh used
such a device to highlight the artificiality of *Léocadia's*
pink world: the black velvet curtain of the Michodière
Theatre opened on a tulle drop-curtain which for
several instants colored each tableau with its haze of
pure make-believe. The intricate framing devices of
Madame de . . . stress the artificiality implicit in all of
Anouilh's works. Here the curtain opens on a backdrop depicting the façade of a *fin-de-siècle* mansion,
made to appear like a little theatre within the theatre.
In front of the backdrop is a grand piano, displayed
as if for a recital. A delicate youth in evening dress

strolls up to the piano and plays some dated music, while the backdrop rises on a scrim curtain, behind which are to be seen the actors. The young man now begins nonchalantly narrating the story, and as he gracefully yields to the actors, the scrim in turn will rise. Even the music has discreetly added to the sham, just as it does in other plays: *Léocadia* has a background waltz by Poulenc; the false ending of *Le Voyageur sans bagage* has a musical accompaniment by Milhaud; the artificiality of *Le Bal des voleurs* is underscored by a clarinetist who freely mingles with the cast; and, of course, *L'Orchestre is* a recital.[1]

Once the stage is bared, we notice that the lighting is contributing to the make-believe. At a time when directors are relying more and more on the spotlight, with its stark modeling and chiaroscuro effects, Anouilh chooses to bathe his sets in the total brightness of floodlights. He has particular recourse to the footlights, whose mere mention is evocative of the gay and glowing sun-drenched theatre of yesterday. In fact, at a recent production of *L'Hurluberlu,* the dramatist's original director and set designer had footlights expressly installed in a modern Frankfort theatre.

Gazing at the stage, we behold settings unlike anything we are accustomed to seeing on our own side of the proscenium; for here on the boards everything is two-dimensional, pictorial, artificial. "A set as unrealistic as possible" (*Episode de la vie d'un auteur*); "Nothing seems real in either décor" (*La Grotte*):

1. The score for *Le Bal des voleurs* was written by Darius Milhaud, that for *La Petite Molière* by Jean-Michel Damase, and that for *L'Orchestre* by Georges Van Parys. In addition, in 1948 Anouilh wrote a scenario, "Les Demoiselles de la Nuit," for Rolland Petit's Ballets de Paris, with music by Jean Françaix.

such instructions might well have been repeated in every text. Often the settings are from another era— turn-of-the-century décors, whose dated features the designer has playfully emphasized with a thousand liberties. Or the curtain may reveal a contemporary scene, a box set that is but a caricature of the naturalistic box set, for all is dummy and deception. While most box sets are covered in a large-patterned commercial wallpaper, Anouilh's flats are painted—and painted with patterns so oversized and mannered that the spectator cannot escape their falseness. The décor of *La Répétition* is an abandoned château. A huge mirror, lamps, and wood trimmings are all *painted* on its gray walls; in the background are a partly hung curtain, a ladder, a red screen; in the foreground are the actors in elegant Louis XV costumes and contemporary haircuts. "The setting was like an engraving, like a drawing," explained designer Jean-Denis Malclès at an interview; the characters were disconcerting, the total effect bizarre, obviously contrived. The sundry sets of *La Petite Molière* are also mainly and plainly dummies, even as they depict such hallowed precincts as the confessional or the conjugal bed. In *Madame de . . .*, the most stylized of Anouilh's works, not only are exteriors and interiors reduced to canvas, but so, too, on occasion, are the actors themselves. And when Anouilh's décors are not so patently artificial, they are often only barely suggested: a series of vertical lines in *Becket* are alternately the pillars of a cathedral and the trees of a forest; *Antigone* is played before a neutral black backdrop; and *L'Alouette* (originally intended to be played before a gray backdrop but changed because of the dismal effect this produced) has an equally artificial and ill-defined décor, comprising a grandstand, a spare wooden throne, a picket fence, and a series of faggots.

Looking at any of these settings more closely, we see that the various properties contribute to the theatricality: they, too, have that drawn quality. Malclès writes that Anouilh will sometimes reject a piece of furniture or a costume fabric with the simple phrase "It's not 'theatre.' " The fact is, he adds, every single object placed on an Anouilh set "is intended to convey a feeling of pictorial transposition."[2] Frequently, even the flea market will not yield furniture of this quality, and the required pieces must be designed and manufactured specially—a procedure most uncommon in Paris theatres.

Naturally, costumes, too, set off the artificiality of this universe. Very rarely has the playwright specified within a text that an article of clothing is to be "false" or "bizarre" (as he did in *Cécile* and *Léocadia*), but it is his unvarying intention that costumes look as "theatre-like" as possible. The designer has caught a pictorial quality by working with flat, mat fabrics. But to project the more elusive stagy quality, he has had to design clothes that actually *look* like costumes, that are vaguely reminiscent of the improvised costumes amateurs might wear. It is as if children were pretending, and, having appropriated various odds and ends for costumes, were now calling upon their spectators to round out the creation with their own imaginations. Malclès illustrates with two anecdotes. For several weeks before the opening of *Becket,* Daniel Ivernel rehearsed his role of Henry Plantagenet by using for his cape an old scrap of backstage curtain. For Jean

2. Jean-Denis Malclès, "Avec Jean Anouilh," Renaud-Barrault *Cahiers, 26,* 40.

Anouilh this improvised cape, by demanding greater play from the spectator's imagination, was an essentially more theatrical costume than the subsequent real one; and his regret, when the actor was ultimately obliged to abandon his "play" cape, was only slighly facetious. *Pauvre Bitos* is situated in the present, and its cast is made up in eighteenth-century style only above their necks. Malclès had originally hoped to clothe them in contemporary tuxedos, but he found such dress to be too banal and dull, too true to life, to cast the necessary sparkle of theatricality. He added a jabot and laced cuffs to the authentic tuxedo, but it still didn't "take": the clothes still looked as if they had been purchased around the corner, the characters did not seem to be stepping out of a picture book, their silhouettes were not "drawn." Finally, Malclès had to design tuxedos specially for the play, and by chance the long, tightly closed, narrow-lapelled jackets reaching to the mid-thigh had the cut of eighteenth-century dress. The tailor who made them was aghast, but the world of theatricality was overjoyed.

Before a word of dialogue is spoken, the spectators understand that the production is geared to artificiality. As the drama itself at last begins to unfold, they wonder whether the acting, too, will be theatrical: Will it be stylized, remote, declamatory, burlesque? Actually, there is no one particular acting style consentient with theatricalism. Some of the most boldly theatricalist productions may be interpreted with stark inner or psychological realism. Jean Anouilh's own position is complex. In keeping with that indefinable transposed quality he seeks throughout his work, he wishes—in theory, at least—the performance to be dancing, droll, poetic, and graceful. At the Bordeaux

summer festival in 1961, he attended a performance
of Jean-Michel Damase's lyric opera *Colombe* (Damase
had already composed a delightful background score
for *La Petite Molière*). And as he heard his own intact
dialogues set to music, Anouilh was thrilled: here at
last was the rare tonality, the magical transposition he
had always imagined that his dialogues should have,
and he vowed (Malclès tells us) to write one day for
the opera. Unfortunately, not everyone shared the
librettist's enthusiasm for *Colombe*. Paris received the
opera, in June 1963, respectfully but cooly. Our own
impression before Damase's dreamlike, undulating,
atmospheric score was that while it certainly reflected
the transposed quality of the dialogues and lifted them
to a realm of higher beauty, it sapped their vitality,
pungency, and humor. Perhaps the old clichés about
writing's aspiring to the condition of poetry are true
after all. Perhaps the art toward which Jean Anouilh
aspires is more abstract and beautiful than the prosaic
barbs and blunders of human encounters.

But of more significance than the operatic ideal is
theatrical necessity: in spite of the author's passion for
transposing, the plays themselves have *not* been interpreted with extreme and obvious poetry. With the
exception of the historical second act of *Pauvre Bitos,*
when the actors were summoned to talk in a singsong,
purportedly eighteenth-century intonation, Anouilh
has never really expected his interpreters to perform
in an artificial, freely poetic style. Their tone may
smack of red curtains and footlights, but their roles
must be human and psychologically true. We recall
that the author usually expends great effort working
with the actors to "compose" each character—that is, to
reconstruct his personality and project it with enough

realism to give the role substance and emotional thrust in the auditorium. Perhaps Anouilh is too much a man of the theatre to sacrifice his art to his impact. As a result, the interpretations have a certain ambiguity. The injunction to the lead of *La Valse des toréadors* bears repeating: "both a marionette, as the author asked him to be, and a human character." The formula warrants special repeating to Americans, who tend to dwell on the hidden, bitter values of these plays and ignore their pink sugar-coating. In Paris, Anouilh's plays are invariably briskly paced and tinged with slapstick, because they *are* comedies and are offered as such. We know that Samuel Beckett intended *Waiting for Godot* to be staged as a direful tragedy, but Jean Anouilh exhibits his black farces as farces.

Implicit in the above remarks is the fact that Anouilh is his own director. Although it was not until *Becket,* in 1959, that he formally received credit for directing (his staging of *L'Alouette* in 1953 was unsigned), and although even now he shares official credits with Roland Piétri, colleagues attest to the dramatist's long-standing and incisive efforts in all the phases of staging, from choosing the actors to choosing the properties, from attending rehearsals to attending costume fittings. "There are no details in which we could get along without him," declared Piétri.[3] It seems reasonable that enterprising of this sort should have nettled an occasional associate. Rumors to the effect circulated during the 1950–51 season, especially as Anouilh attempted to relieve Jean Servais of his role of Héro the day before *La Répétition* was due to open ("*La Répétition,* which was a triumph, was

3. Roland Piétri, "Avec Jean Anouilh," ibid., p. 39.

forged in pain," Barrault subsequently admitted, re-
ferring to Anouilh's interventions in his production
of the play).[4] In general, however, the playwright's associates have appreciated working with an artist who
knows exactly what he wants. Malclès has put it this
way:

> From the outset there are long discussions in
> which every theme and idea is jotted down on
> sheets of drawing paper. Indeed, with Jean
> Anouilh (who draws well) explanations are clear,
> suggestions become concrete forms and are not
> left as dangerously vague words; there cannot be
> any misunderstandings: you can reply by another
> drawing. That is an extremely pleasant and very
> practical way to advance a discussion.[5]

Although Anouilh's interpreters have included at
one time or another such figures as the Pitoëffs, Jean-
Louis Barrault, and Pierre Fresnay, the total number
has remained quite limited. For ten years (1938–47)
he worked almost exclusively with André Barsacq at
the Atelier Theatre; since 1948, most of the plays have
been produced at the Comédie des Champs-Elysées in
conjunction with Piétri and Malclès. Anouilh has
shown a similar predilection to work with certain actors: Christian Lude, Maurice Jacquemont, François-
Marie, Gerard Darrieu, Marie Leduc, and, especially,
Michel Bouquet and Marcel Perès are among the actors who have appeared in so many plays that they
have come to constitute a virtual "Anouilh caravan."

4. Jean-Louis Barrault, "Depuis Chaptal . . . ," ibid., p. 47; see
also, Claude Brule, "Anouilh toujours sauvage," Opéra (Jan. 24,
1951).

5. Malclès, Cahiers, 26, 40.

And it is plain that the unofficial troupe, with an occasional role tailored for one of its members, has been able to work closely, harmoniously, and effectively.

One of the more fascinating aspects of Anouilh's dramaturgy is the enormous importance he attributes to costumes. He seems to have mastered their employment early in his career. In *Jézabel,* one of the first plays, the hero imagines his embarrassment at the spectacle of his father dressed in a top hat; just a few years later, in *La Sauvage,* an equally boorish parent, rigged in tux and topper, actually comes on stage to precipitate a most heart-rending scene. In *Jézabel* Marc has a grandiose vision of his fiancée in her bridal gown; in several subsequent plays we actually see the tarnished heroine physically bearing the symbolic gown of purity. Again in *Jézabel,* Marc's mother makes a fleeting appearance on stage, and father and son proceed, very clumsily, to discuss the vulgarity and negligence of her attire. In the plays that follow, costumes speak for themselves, and their speech is often stunning. "Don't you believe in anything on this earth?" Mlle. Supo asks Ornifle; "I believe that two and two don't make four," he snaps, donning the wig of Alceste precisely as he parodies Don Juan (*PG,* p. 290). In *Colombe* the heroine welcomes home her husband with a kittenish "How do you like my little hazel ensemble?" and we immediately know she has accepted the gift proposed earlier by Desfournettes—and collectible only after a stint on his "casting couch." The scene builds and Julien finally accuses his wife of infidelity; she steps from behind her dressing-room screen, where she is preparing for the evening's performance, and in her very French underwear, hands crossed over a nearly naked bosom, asks innocently,

"Why darling, what do you mean?" (*PB*, p. 265). The
effect is devastating.

By tradition, dress is one of the simplest characterizing devices at a playwright's disposal. No more subtle
than a clown's motley and flour are Ornifle's blood-
red robe, Mlle. Supo's mousey gray blouse and skirt,
or, for that matter, the plain white linen frocks of the
various young heroines. Just a shade more subtle is
the verbal characterizing by means of costume, for example Héro's cynical evocation of Lucile's and the
Count's idyl: "He'll order a nice 'Young Executive'
suit at the department store and come wait for you outside your office at five o'clock, clutching a ten-cent
bouquet of violets" (*PB*, p. 452). According to Malclès,
each stage costume arises from and faithfully mirrors
each stage character. In other words, just as every member of the cast may enjoy his own rhythm and idiom,
so, too, is he stamped with a personal and unique
silhouette. The goal is to give everyone a costume "that
could be worn only by him," to create an effect "as if
it couldn't be otherwise."[6] Malclès has denied any effort to ennoble or ridicule the characters through
dress. And yet, when we turn to a few of the texts, we
have the distinct impression that the dramatist himself
has costumed his characters with an eye to ennobling
or, much more often, ridiculing them.

For years the staging of *Antigone* intrigued observers and precipitated a variety of interpretations. Some
saw in the modern evening-dress nothing but an at-
tention-getting theatrical device. Others pointed out
the parallel to French classical tragedy, whose Greek
and Roman characters once appeared in seventeenth-

6. Ibid., p. 41.

century attire. It remained for the director-designer
André Barsacq to reveal the true intention some fifteen years after the original production:

> Actually, there was nothing premeditated about
> this desire for modernism. We had only sought
> costumes that might constitute something of a
> uniform for our interpreters, and in this way ar-
> rived at the idea of evening dress. The king and
> all the members of the royal family wore dress-
> coats, Antigone and her sister Ismène, long white
> and black dresses, and the guards, tuxedos, over
> which they had placed black oilskins. This sym-
> phony of black and white gave a rare unity to the
> performance, and its sobriety added to the im-
> pression of grandeur emitting from the whole
> spectacle.[7]

It would seem, then, that the impelling notion was
that of elevating the tone, of imparting a degree of
dignity to the characters by means of the costumes.

If here Anouilh has exploited costuming to ennoble
his creatures, elsewhere he has proceeded with even
more ingenuity to ridicule them. Often a character
finds himself decked in some preposterous garb, just
as he is being attacked or mocked. The cherished
Molière, for example, is made to recite from *Dom
Garcie,* his early, unsuccessful tragedy, "in shirt sleeves,
with a shirt tail hanging out of his breeches from behind, rigged moreover in a plumed Roman helmet
. . . declaiming, as serious as he is ridiculous" (*MO*,
p. 13). By means of this grotesque tableau, Anouilh is

---

7. André Barsacq, "A l'Atelier pendant près de quinze ans,"
Renaúd-Barrault *Cahiers*, 26, 34–35.

saying concretely and theatrically, "Molière, the writer of serious plays, was a fool."

On several occasions Anouilh has gone even further, employing costumes less as a characterizing device than as a distinct instrument of torture. In the third act of *L'Hurluberlu* the General is subjected to a succession of nearly mortal blows from his wife, his daughter, and his daughter's fiancé. How is he dressed during these assaults? Not as he was during the first part of the play, in knickerbockers, boots, and lounging jacket. Anouilh has seen fit to deck him in a "vaguely grotesque" (*HU*, p. 122) costume, ostensibly because several members of the cast are rehearsing a nineteenth-century Spanish comedy. In the original Paris production this meant that the General was wearing pastel lavender trousers, a knee-length, single-buttoned, tightly waisted, lavender-blue frock coat, lace cuffs, jabot, and top hat. His wife, Aglaé, on the other hand, was far from grotesque. For the same amateur production she was wearing a beautiful, long white dress —"A Spanish lady out of Goya," defines Anouilh— while the General's other two antagonists were in contemporary attire. According to Malclès, no attempt was made to reproduce authentic Spanish costuming; rather, the General was clothed in just the sort of costume a provincial amateur might concoct as appropriate for an historical Spanish play. Hence, if he was meant to appear ridiculous, it was only insofar as a retired general so dressed would be out of his element. And yet, as instants later Aglaé tries to lead her bearish, wretchedly clumsy husband in a waltz step—she, graceful in her flowing white dress; he, still "wearing the crown of thorns and the purple robe"—we can virtually hear Anouilh jeering from off stage, "Behold the clown!"

For his venomous portrayal of André Bitos the dramatist exploited costuming almost to the point of having a sans-culotte wander about the stage in a nightmare of pantsless ridicule. The guests at this *dîner de têtes* are attired in what we have gathered from *Antigone* to be the dignity-inspiring costume of evening dress. Into this patrician setting pops Bitos, sporting not only a much-too-tight topcoat and tiny derby (the same outfit, by the way, that Anouilh devised for his up-dated Tartuffe) but also a full-length, bona-fide, eighteenth-century costume. Everyone immediately seizes the quaintness of his position—including Bitos himself, poor devil, who would fain make a break for it and return in conventional dress. But host Maxime forbids, and throughout the play this moral pariah will project pictorially as an outcast amidst elegance.

During the historical second act of *Pauvre Bitos* Anouilh again exploits costumes by contrasting the cramped viciousness of Robespierre to the relaxed worldliness of his fellow revolutionaries. As the act closes and the unbalanced Robespierre glides from the puritanical into the tyrannical, Anouilh calls for him to put back on the narrow topcoat and derby of Bitos the civil servant, thereby making more pertinent to the twentieth-century audience Robespierre's terrifying program for moral redress, his downstage diatribe against the vein of facility and insouciance in the French people. In the final act we are treated to the spectacle of Bitos in from the rain, huddled in "a sort of ridiculous curtain," very soggy and very pitiful—and, as he gets sodden with whisky, "more and more

the Roman Caesar, draped in his curtain" (*PG*, p. 491).
Finally, André unwittingly rips open the seat of his
trousers: Does he lose his head? No, he has the butler
repair, most gingerly, to be sure, the damage to what
Anouilh several moments before has termed "that
ridiculous part of [his] body" (ibid., p. 439). While
he is in this graceless posture, enters Victoire, the
woman who was refused to him in marriage that very
day. Mortified, Bitos is made to finish his play as would
a clown, his hands protecting his bottom. And once
again we distinctly hear the author jeering from the
wings—this time, "Ecce clunis!"

Anouilh's stage creatures are not just ridiculed, en-
nobled, and characterized by their costumes; at times
they are actually dominated by them. A piece of clothing for such hypersensitive people may hold vast affec-
tive powers and inhibit or induce all sorts of behavior.
As was the case earlier with the tendency to self-drama-
tize, here again the artist may well have projected his
own sensitivity into the hearts of his characters.

Certainly, as a director, Anouilh has shown himself
to be highly perceptive in regard to dress. His first
venture with a nonoriginal work came in 1960 when
he staged *Tartuffe* at the Comédie des Champs-Elysées.
Convinced that seventeenth-century costumes would
alienate a contemporary audience, Anouilh shifted the
action to La Belle Epoque—last bastion of the pious-
ness and parental authority so vital to the plot. While
his production was favorably received by the press
(Tartuffe was another Bitos: a son of the poor, fighting
for survival, and sincerely in love with Elmire),[8] his

8. Anouilh has ably defended his interpretation of Molière in
Le Songe du critique, a one-act impromptu performed together with
Tartuffe. One of his leading actors, François Périer, has offered addi-

reasoned modernism was dismissed as a piece of gratuitous theatricality. And considering that Anouilh
evidently had no misgivings lest medieval costumes
alienate audiences of *L'Alouette* and *Becket,* one may
well question his good faith. Still, the man's hypersensitivity to dress cannot be questioned. When casting for one of his own works, he will ask a prospective
actor to put on a false mustache or a derby. With something to hide behind, the actor will no longer have his
"everyday face"; the paraphernalia will facilitate his
flight from reality into the world of theatre; he will
thus raise the tone of his performance—in a word, he
will act. Later, during rehearsals, as the director
hastens to establish the silhouette or essence of each
role, again he shows a peculiar reliance on costume.
In *La Foire d'empoigne,* for example, actor Paul
Meurisse had the spiny task of transforming himself
into two contradictory personages, Napoleon and
Louis XVIII. At Anouilh's suggestion, from the first
rehearsals, the actor read his lines wearing either
Napoleon's famous hat or a vague restoration wig, the
better to define and create each role.

Proceeding just a step further to the actor-characters
who abound in Anouilh's texts, one encounters a similar dependence on costume and appurtenance. Vincent, for example, the elderly trouper of *Eurydice,*
cannot play a certain part without his goatee. Actually,
even Shakespeare is not spared: in *La Nuit des rois*
(Anouilh's adaptation of *Twelfth Night*) the clown
pretends to be a curate in order to dupe Malvolio, who

tional remarks (*Les Nouvelles littéraires,* Nov. 10, 1960). In October
1962 Anouilh and Piétri staged Roger Vitrac's *Victor ou les enfants
au pouvoir;* the production was acclaimed.

is imprisoned just off stage. Reproached that he might have dispensed with his disguise of curate's gown and beard because Malvolio was not even able to see him, Shakespeare's clown says nothing. But Anouilh's quickly retorts, "Wrong! Without the robe and the beard I should not have found the right tone" (IV.2).

Other of the playwright's characters besides those who portray actors exhibit this dependency. In Anouilh's so-called film scenario *Cavalcade d'amour*, a father wishes to have a heart-to-heart talk with his daughter. "I'll help you to look like a father," she says. "What you really need is gravity—something you just don't have right now. What can we do to make you look serious?" She picks up a high silk hat, crowns her father, and backs off. "There! Now you can play me your scene; you look just like M. Duval in *La Dame aux camélias*" (p. 21). In *Ardèle* the General brags that for his skirmish with the hunchback, he cleverly reinforced his position by wearing a full-dress uniform complete with decorations. Thomas à Becket, anticipating his death, dons almost compulsively the formal attire of an archbishop. And as we witness the striking tableau of his martyrdom, we are barely conscious of the genius of the playwright who has transposed pictorially the hero's courage and intransigence; for, having overcome the vanities of asceticism and the facilities of a holy retreat, Becket now understands that he can truly embody the Archbishop of Canterbury neither by effacing himself beneath the monk's robe and haircloth nor by isolating himself in a ritual intended for others. Rather, he must attack unflinchingly his every duty as archbishop, bear the responsibility of his immense powers, and display the costume emblematic of his office. He thus resembles Jeanne d'Arc,

who, after a momentary aberration, exultingly becomes "true to herself forever," and calls in the same
breath for her men's breeches and the stake.

Even more fascinating are the characters who are
so oddly dependent on staging that suddenly, even in
the midst of an act, they balk and skittishly refuse to
play out a scene for want of proper costuming. Marc,
the tormented young hero of *Jézabel,* wishes to confide
something important to his mother, but she, oblivious
to the youth's maladroit advances, just primps before
her mirror and idly asks how he likes her new coiffure.
"How much easier it would be to talk to you if you
weren't dyed Venetian blond," Marc says to the gaud-
ily dressed woman. Then, on the brink of emptying his
heart, he cries, "Sit down. At least take off your little
beret. Yes, take it off. I'll sit on the floor. Here, I'm
putting my head on your lap as I did when I was little.
I'm unhappy, mother, and it's because of you. . . . For
a long time, for ten years perhaps, I've dreamed that
I'd talk to you this way" (*NPN,* pp. 44–45). What is
the effect of the foregoing dialogue? Marc's reproaches
have, of course, set off the character of his mother—
her egotism, coquetry, and indifference.[9] But without
having advanced the action one iota, the playwright
has set the scene for a dramatic disclosure and created
a measure of suspense. The spectator is unaware of
Marc's problems, but he feels they must be important
enough to merit these finicky preparations. And if

9. Her preoccupation with clothing is basically a preoccupation
with appearances, and calls to mind other of Anouilh's sorry puppets:
Eurydice's mother can describe moments of past joy only in terms
of the clothes she was wearing; Adeline, in *Y'Avait un Prisonnier,*
associates her husband's incarceration with the fur piece she was
wearing when he left; etc.

Marc has set the scene for his own benefit, it is really
each spectator who is taken in with him—not so much
because mother and son strike up a touching pose
downstage as because this pose is artificial, because the
spectator, even more than Marc, feels the pathos in
that futile playing out of fictitious dreams. Indeed, in
trying to strip his mother of one inappropriate mask
(her pale blond hair and girl's beret), the hero has
gone on to impose another equally theatrical mask:
the childish, artificial pose of mother and son.

At the close of the second act of *Ornifle,* young
Fabrice slips onto the stage. Quickly and nervously,
he explains his mission: he will avenge his dishonored
mother by murdering the rake who years ago seduced
her: Ornifle. Unfortunately, but with dogged French
logic, this rake is his own father. The situation may be
awkward, but the dialogue is light and witty. Abruptly,
Fabrice draws a pistol, aims it at an astonished Ornifle
(who all this while is costumed as the Misanthrope in
preparation for a masked ball), and says,

> Take off your wig. You are ridiculous. I can't kill
> you like that. . . . Back up, I don't want to kill
> you point blank, you know. And take off your wig.
> I don't want you to look ridiculous when you're
> dead, either. After all, you're my father. (*He cries
> suddenly:*) Come on, take it off, it's in your own
> interest! I can't wait any longer. You won't take
> the wig off? Very well! I'll kill you as you are. And
> too bad for you! You'll be ridiculous!
>
> [*PG,* pp. 297, 299]

Just as Marc had done, Fabrice, too, is enacting a vision
he has nurtured for years: "If you think it's funny to
have to kill someone! Only . . . I took an oath. When
I was ten. And I'm in the habit of keeping my word!"

It is not mere capriciousness that dictates such concern about costume: it is an awareness that at last he
is playing out a momentous scene. As a matter of fact,
play-acting is about all Fabrice can do: at present he
is performing as the Avenger of Family Honor; in an
earlier chapter we saw him as the Reproachful Lover;
and soon he will do the Selfless Physician. But whereas
it was a craving for maternal affection that led Marc,
very understandably, to prefer black dress, gray hair,
and motherly pose, the fulfillment of Fabrice's ven-
geance is utterly unrelated to wigs. The youth's fussi-
ness is absurd—whence, in part, the humor. This same
sort of absurd dependence upon costume was used in
one of Anouilh's first plays, *Le Bal des voleurs,* when
Eva told the disguised pickpocket, Hector, she was
incapable of loving him unless he reappeared in the
costume he first wore before her.

In *Ornifle* the humor is largely due to the actual
physical appearance of the hero: he certainly *is* ridiculous, thus held at gunpoint, this suave, overbearing
cynic, his black, close-cropped beard now partly
covered by a curled and powdered wig. And that
ridiculousness is emphasized by Fabrice's highly theatrical observations. We can almost hear the boy panting desperately, "How can I play at Orestes when
you're trying to play Molière?" Two contrasting
theatres collide, two hams cross and bring down the
apogee of farce: the avenger fires but his pistol does
not; the villain passes out from fright; son rushes to
prostrate father, listens for his heartbeat, consults a
noble vade mecum, and rattles off bursts of medical
double-talk, as Mlle. Supo charges onto the scene,
naked under a curious red tablecloth, the costume she
has concocted to play out her sexual sacrifice to Ornifle.
And the curtain falls.

Conclusion

"What is the origin of your theatre?" Jean
Anouilh was asked in 1951. "You know," he replied,
"it seems to me that everything is in *Le Bal des voleurs*.
My characters, my themes. Inspiration is just an em-
broidery on immutable figures."[1] He might have
added that the origin of his dramatic technique can
also be traced to *Le Bal des voleurs*, where the ridicu-
lously costumed imposters dance a ballet of pretense,
where already visible are instances of role-playing,
self-dramatizing, and scene-spinning, and where the
central figure "plays at intrigues" and occasionally
wavers between caricature and character. Indeed, just
about everything seems to be here—everything, that
is, except substance; for the twenty-two-year-old author was aiming at the boulevards when he wrote this
"pièce rose," and what he created was little more than
a flimsy entertainment. All the substance during those
early years was going instead into the "pièces noires,"
into the black, naturalistic melodramas *L'Hermine*
and *Jézabel*.

The broader origins of Anouilh's dramaturgy are
anterior even to *Le Bal des voleurs*. Before he had
written what were to be his first performed plays, the

1. *Arts* (Nov. 16, 1951).

youth was smitten. He was already hopelessly and irrevocably in love with the theatre—so much so, in fact, that, outdoing Shakespeare, he really *saw* the world as a stage, he really *sensed* his fellow men as players. In short, he was confusing theatre and life. An outlook like this could not but color his dramatic writings: it led to a self-consciousness and a preciosity that were forgivable in *Le Bal des voleurs* but were quite out of place in the early "pièces noires."

Origins may be vague, but turning points are not, and the critical moment in the development of Anouilh's dramaturgy came in the mid-30s when, under the influence of Giraudoux and Pirandello— but mainly bending to his own predilections—he adopted the theatricalist æsthetic of the *jeu*. Theatricalism enabled Anouilh to synthesize his ill-assorted tendencies. It preached that a play should openly exploit, not hide, conventions and theatricality. In an instant all his self-consciousness and preciosity were legitimized: Jean Anouilh could now "play the theatrical game with sincerity."[2] Theatricalism virtually redefined drama as a transposition of life into theatre; and henceforth the youth's exaggerated Shakespearean outlook was to be an asset. For years he had cherished the very trappings of the stage, and now he would follow through, blithely—and effectively—transposing life's events into stock situations, transposing human characters into stage caricatures, transposing visible reality into scenic décor, transposing (or, more accurately, elevating) everyday talk into the language of the stage. But most important of all, the theatricalist æsthetic taught the author that artifice and showman-

2. Les Sept, *La Gazette des lettres* (Dec. 1950), p. 7.

ship are the backbone of *all* drama, even of the most profound. Consequently, he was able to reconcile his taste for theatrics and buffoonery to a drama of substance: in an instant he had learned to wed the frivolous form of his first "pièce rose" to the meaningful content of early "pièces noires." This was a key step, for had Anouilh's technique evolved in a trajectory from, let us say, *Le Bal des voleurs,* it might still have attained a certain virtuosity, but the plays themselves would have remained hollow and sterile. The writer would have found himself courting that same oblivion haunted by previous master technicians and carpenters, whose creations were void of ideas, poetry, or even memorable characters.

What precisely was the debt to Giraudoux and Pirandello? Anouilh has described his entrancement at the first Giraudoux production, *Siegfried.*[3] Until that spring evening, the eighteen-year-old devotee had seen only well-made plays, plays whose forte was the very triteness of their situation, the very prosaism of their language. And here in *Siegfried* was their antithesis: a fanciful story told in language that fairly sparkled and danced and breathed with poetry. It is this poetry and fancifulness which were Giraudoux's gifts to Anouilh. Assuredly, it was easier for Anouilh to copy the Limousin's fantasy of situation than to match his singular style, but it was Giraudoux, nevertheless, who set him on the linguistic path upward.

The role of Pirandello is less clear. Thomas Bishop, in his study of *Pirandello and the French Theatre,* traced the Italian's influence on two generations of French dramatists and found it reflected most clearly

3. Anouilh, "A Jean Giraudoux," *La Chronique de Paris* (Feb. 1944).

in Anouilh. "Anouilh's great debt to Pirandello," he concluded, "is in the themes that he has adapted and in the Pirandellian flavor of much of his dialogue and atmosphere."[4] But how many of the themes attributed to Pirandello (among them: relativity of truth, multiplication of personality, notion of roles, split between reality and illusion, between life and form) are not traditional themes of dramatic literature? Could one not reduce, say, Pirandello's theme of multiplicity of personality to that of hypocrisy or of the mask? Would not Anouilh in this instance be taking his cue from Molière, Marivaux, and Musset rather than from Pirandello? And then, are Anouilh's dramas really Pirandellian in atmosphere? Could anything be further removed from the Italian's metaphysical meshwork than Anouilh's intensely alive dialogues?

Yet the fact remains that Anouilh himself once said, "I have come from Pirandello, that's all. 'Six Characters in Search of an Author.' I haven't invented a thing since."[5] It is likely that what Anouilh really found in Pirandello was encouragement for his own infatuation with theatre. From his precocious beginnings, the Frenchman had been intoxicated with "playing theatre," and Pirandello's most popular works were paeans to the process of dramatic creation. *Six Characters in Search of an Author* not merely represented for Anouilh the asphyxiation of the well-made play but marked the ascendancy of theatre itself over the contents of theatre.

Fortunately, Anouilh was able to see beyond the dazzling first truths of Pirandello and to escape the

4. Bishop, *Pirandello and the French Theatre* New York, New York University Press, 1960), p. 118.

5. *Opéra* (Feb. 14, 1951).

blind alley of "playing at playmaking."[6] His theatricalist vision mellowed and grew more sophisticated.
The characters learned to control their bent for self-
dramatizing and to reserve it mainly for humor. They
pictured themselves and others in set roles and exploited this concept for farce or, more subtly, for
tragedy. They talked about events—some recalled,
others just imagined—as if each event were a startling
scene from a play or film. Their very cerebration became scenic. And these are the traits which truly distinguish Anouilh's dramaturgy.

Continuing to toy with his material, Anouilh took
more and more liberties, fragmenting the action, con-
joining disparate moods. The distinction between
"pièces roses" and "pièces noires" (even from the start
somewhat arbitrary) was now abandoned altogether;
the plays became bicolor: pink without, black within.
Anouilh had always been a bit of a *sauvage,* and once
beyond the anguished introspection of his youth he
was less and less prone to speak forth directly on mat-
ters that sorely touched him. Soon he was toying with
his subject only up to a certain point, and then swiftly pirouetting away, the better to conceal his black
truths, just as the French classicists had done, he said,
and Molière in particular. As he continued to perfect
his humor of compensation, emphasizing the pastel
veil of laughter rather than the black core of meaning,
the artist now understood he was being virile, laughing
at the human predicament rather than weeping over
it—or doing anything about it. Even though it seemed
to be predicated upon man's infinite capacity for
rottenness, his vision of humanity had never been truly

6. Gassner, *Form and Idea,* p. 143.

despairing. There had always been heroes in his works, and, grim as their fate may have been, their mere presence had proved that some people—a whole race of them, in fact—could rise above facility and self-deception. As he grew older and the vision confirmed itself, it began to appear, if only cumulatively, unpleasant, even offensive, to playgoers. The ideal still burned, to be sure, but dimly now, on a far horizon, and not for consumption in this world.

As a man of rigor, Anouilh could not tamper with truth, no matter how black or how repellent. As a man of the theatre, however, he was able to attenuate that truth by thickening the pink cloud of theatricality about it. In the 1960s, as the vision has darkened somewhat with *La Grotte* and *L'Orchestre,* the cloud has accordingly brightened, and theatricality has become almost as rosy and obvious and precious as it had been long ago. But Anouilh's posture remains the same. For years he has been a moralist, ransoming life with the spectacle of its own vices; a comic, cheating death with laughter; a showman, strutting the boards with pink tights . . . and black bottom.

Appendix

Chronology of Anouilh's plays: when written (if known, in parentheses) and when first performed in Paris.

Humulus le muet (1929?). Not performed.

Mandarine (1929), Feb. 1933, Théâtre de l'Athénée.

L'Hermine (1931), April 26, 1932, Théâtre de l'Oeuvre, directed by Lugné-Poe.

Jézabel (1932). Not performed.

Le Bal des voleurs (1932), Sept. 17, 1938, Théâtre des Arts, directed by André Barsacq.

La Sauvage (1934), Jan. 10, 1938, Théâtre des Mathurins, directed by Georges Pitoëff.

Y'Avait un Prisonnier, March 21, 1935, Théâtre des Ambassadeurs, directed by Marie Bell.

Le Voyageur sans bagage (1936), Feb. 16, 1937, Théâtre des Mathurins, directed by Georges Pitoëff.

Le Rendez-vous de Senlis (1937), Jan. 1941, Théâtre de l'Atelier, directed by André Barsacq.

Léocadia (1939), Nov. 1940, Théâtre de la Michodière.

Eurydice (1941), Dec. 18, 1942, Théâtre de l'Atelier, directed by André Barsacq.

Oreste (1942?). Not performed.

Antigone (1942), Feb. 4, 1944, Théâtre de l'Atelier, directed by André Barsacq.

Roméo et Jeannette (1945), Dec. 3, 1946, Théâtre de l'Atelier, directed by André Barsacq.

Médée (1946), March 26, 1953, Théâtre de l'Atelier, directed by André Barsacq.

L'Invitation au château (1946), Nov. 4, 1947, Théâtre de l'Atelier, directed by André Barsacq.

Ardèle ou la marguerite, Nov. 3, 1948, Comédie des Champs-Elysées, directed by Roland Piétri.

Episode de la vie d'un auteur, Nov. 3, 1948, with *Ardèle.*

La Répétition ou l'amour puni, Oct. 25, 1950, Théâtre Marigny, directed by Jean-Louis Barrault.

Colombe, Feb. 11, 1951, Théâtre de l'Atelier, directed by André Barsacq.

Cécile, Oct. 29, 1954, Comédie des Champs-Elysées, directed by Roland Piétri.

La Valse des toréadors, Jan. 9, 1952, Comédie des Champs-Elysées, directed by Roland Piétri.

L'Alouette (1952), Oct. 14, 1953, Théâtre Montparnasse, directed by Jean Anouilh.

Ornifle ou le courant d'air, Nov. 3, 1955, Comédie des Champs-Elysées.

Pauvre Bitos ou le dîner de têtes, Oct. 11, 1956, Théâtre Montparnasse, directed by Roland Piétri.

L'Hurluberlu ou le réactionnaire amoureux (1958?), Feb. 5, 1959, Comédie des Champs-Elysées, directed by Roland Piétri.

La Petite Molière, Nov. 12, 1959, Odéon-Théâtre de France, directed by Jean-Louis Barrault (first performed in Bordeaux, June 1, 1959).

Becket ou l'honneur de Dieu (1958), Oct. 1, 1959, Théâtre Montparnasse, directed by Jean Anouilh and Roland Piétri.

La Foire d'empoigne (1959), Jan. 11, 1962, Comédie des Champs-Elysées, directed by Jean Anouilh and Roland Piétri.

Le Songe du critique, Nov. 5, 1960, Comédie des Champs-Elysées, directed by Jean Anouilh.

La Grotte, Oct. 4, 1961, Théâtre Montparnasse, directed by Jean Anouilh and Roland Piétri.

L'Orchestre, Feb. 10, 1962, Comédie des Champs-Elysées, directed by Jean Anouilh and Roland Piétri.

Bibliography

PUBLISHED PLAYS AND TRANSLATIONS BY
JEAN ANOUILH*

L'Alouette (see *Pièces costumées*).
Antigone (see *Nouvelles Pièces noires*).
Ardèle ou la marguerite (see *Pièces grinçantes*).
Le Bal des voleurs (see *Pièces roses*).
Becket ou l'honneur de Dieu (see *Pièces costumées*).
Cécile ou l'école des pères (see *Pièces brillantes*).
Colombe (see *Pièces brillantes*).
Comme Il vous plaira (see *Trois Comédies de Shake-speare*).
Le Conte d'hiver (see *Trois Comédies de Shakespeare*).
Episode de la vie d'un auteur, Cahiers de la compagnie Madeleine Renaud—Jean-Louis Barrault, Vol. 26, Paris, Julliard, 1959.
Eurydice (see *Pièces noires*).
La Foire d'empoigne (see *Pièces costumées*).
La Grotte, Paris, La Table Ronde, 1961.
L'Hermine, in *Les Oeuvres libres*, No. 151, Paris, Fayard, 1934. (See also, *Pièces noires*).
Humulus le muet (see *Pièces roses*).
L'Hurluberlu ou le réactionnaire amoureux, Paris, La Table Ronde, 1959.
Il est important d'être aimé (adapted by Jean Anouilh

*The editions are those referred to throughout the present book.

and Claude Vincent from *The Importance of Being Earnest* by Oscar Wilde), *L'Avant-Scène*, No. 101, n.d.

L'Invitation au château (see *Pièces brillantes*).

Jézabel (see *Nouvelles Pièces noires*).

Léocadia (see *Pièces roses*).

Médée (see *Nouvelles Pièces noires*).

Nouvelles Pièces noires (*Jézabel, Antigone, Roméo et Jeannette, Médée*), Paris, La Table Ronde, 1947.

La Nuit des rois (see *Trois Comédies de Shakespeare*).

L'Orchestre, in *L'Avant-Scène*, No. 276, 1962.

Oreste, in *La Table ronde*, No. 3, 1945.

Ornifle ou le courant d'air (see *Pièces grinçantes*).

Pauvre Bitos ou le dîner de têtes (see *Pièces grinçantes*).

La Petite Molière (scenario by Jean Anouilh and Roland Laudenbach, dialogues by Jean Anouilh), in *L'Avant-Scène*, No. 210, 1959.

Pièces brillantes (*L'Invitation au château, Colombe, La Répétition ou l'amour puni, Cécile ou l'école des pères*), Paris, La Table Ronde, 1951.

Pièces costumées (*L'Alouette, Becket ou l'honneur de Dieu, La Foire d'empoigne*), Paris, La Table Ronde, 1960.

Pièces grinçantes (*Ardèle ou la marguerite, La Valse des toréadors, Ornifle ou le courant d'air, Pauvre Bitos ou le dîner de têtes*), Paris, La Table Ronde, 1956.

Pièces noires (*L'Hermine, La Sauvage, Le Voyageur sans bagage, Eurydice*), Paris, Calmann-Lévy, 1945.

Pièces roses (*Humulus le muet, Le Bal des voleurs, Le Rendez-vous de Senlis, Léocadia*), Paris, La Table Ronde, 1961.

Le Rendez-vous de Senlis (see *Pièces roses*).

La Répétition ou l'amour puni (see *Pièces brillantes*).

Roméo et Jeannette (see *Nouvelles Pièces noires*).

La Sauvage, in *Les Oeuvres libres*, No. 201, Paris, Fayard, 1938. (See also *Pièces noires*.)

Le Songe du critique, in *L'Avant-Scène*, No. 143, 1961.

Trois Comédies de Shakespeare (*Comme Il vous plaira,*

Le Conte d'hiver, La Nuit des rois, adapted by Jean
  Anouilh and Claude Vincent, Paris, La Table Ronde,
  1952.
La Valse des toréadors (see *Pièces grinçantes*).
Le Voyageur sans bagage, in *La Petite Illustration,* No.
  411, 1937. (See also *Pièces noires.*)
Y'Avait un Prisonnier, in *La Petite Illustration,* No. 370,
  1935.

NONDRAMATIC WRITINGS OF JEAN ANOUILH
(in chronological order)

"Avant-Propos" (to *Le Roi cerf,* by Carlo Gozzi), program
  for *Le Bal des voleurs,* Compagnie des Quatre-Saisons
  de Paris, 1938.
"Monsieur Dullin," program of the Compagnie des
  Quatre-Saisons de Paris, Théâtre de l'Atelier, 1940.
"Mon Cher Pitoëff," *Aujourd 'hui,* Sept. 11, 1940.
"Propos déplacés," *La Gerbe,* Nov. 14, 1940.
Cavalcade d'amour (scenario by Jean Anouilh and Jean
  Aurenche, dialogues by Jean Anouilh), in *Les Films
  inédits,* No. 4, 1941.
"Hommage à Giraudoux," *Chronique de Paris,* Feb. 1944.
"Lettre," in Hubert Gignoux, *Jean Anouilh,* Paris,
  Temps Présent, 1946.
"Hommage à Georges Pitoëff," *Opéra,* May 4, 1949.
"Denis Malclès," program for *La Répétition,* Compagnie
  Madeleine Renaud—Jean-Louis Barrault, 1950.
"Des Ciseaux de papa au 'Sabre de mon père,' " *Opéra,*
  March 7, 1951.
"Ludmilla Pitoëff," *Opéra,* Sept. 9, 1951.
" 'La Valse des toréadors?' Que Voilà Une Bonne Pièce,"
  Le Figaro, Jan. 23, 1952.
"Exposition Paris. Mai 1947," *Michel-Marie Poulain,*
  Paris, Imprimerie de Braun, 1953.
"Godot ou le sketch des pensées de Pascal traité par les
  Fratellini," *Arts,* Feb. 27, 1953.

"Lettre à une jeune fille qui veut faire du théâtre," *Elle,* Jan. 21, 1955.

"La Mort d'une troupe," *Arts,* Oct. 19, 1955.

"Du Chapitre des chaises," *Le Figaro,* April 23, 1956.

"Lettre d'un vieux crocodile à un jeune mousquetaire," *Arts,* May 1, 1957.

"Histoire de M. Mauvette et de la fin du monde" (short story), *Cahiers de la compagnie Madeleine Renaud— Jean-Louis Barrault,* Vol. 26, Paris, Julliard, 1959.

"Présence de Molière," program, Comédie-Française, Jan. 15, 1959 (reprinted in Renaud-Barrault *Cahiers,* Vol. 26.

"Il y a dix ans mourait Charles Dullin," *Le Figaro,* Dec. 12, 1959.

" 'Becket' by Chance," *New York Times,* Oct. 2, 1960.

"Cher Vitrac," *Le Figaro,* Oct. 1, 1962. (Reprinted in *L'Avant-Scène,* No. 276, 1962.)

"Dans Mon Trou de souffleur pour la première fois j'ai eu peur au théâtre," *Paris-Match,* Oct. 20, 1962.

Fables, Lausanne, Guilde du Livre, 1962.

Notes on *Becket* and *La Foire d'empoigne,* in *L'Avant-Scène,* Nos. 282–83, 1963.

INTERVIEWS ACCORDED BY ANOUILH

Les Nouvelles littéraires, March 27, 1937.

Les Nouvelles littéraires, Jan. 10, 1946.

France-Dimanche, Oct. 12, 1950.

Opéra, Feb. 14, 1951.

Arts, Nov. 16, 1951.

New York Times, drama section, Jan. 3, 1954.

Les Nouvelles littéraires, Feb. 5, 1959.

Paris-Match, June 13, 1959.

RECORDINGS OF ANOUILH READING HIS OWN PLAYS

Antigone (16 rpm), La Voix de l'Auteur, No. 1.

Ardèle ou la marguerite (16 rpm), LVA, No. 10.

Cécile ou l'école des pères (33 rpm), LVA, No. 6.
La Foire d'empoigne (16 rpm), LVA, No. 19.
Médée (33 rpm), LVA, No. 31.

FILMS BY ANOUILH (in chronological order)

Les Dégourdis de la onzième, dialogues (coauthor J. Au-
    renche), 1936.
Vous n'avez rien à déclarer, dialogues (coauthor J. Au-
    renche), 1937.
Les Otages, dialogues (coauthor J. Aurenche), 1939.
Le Voyageur sans bagage, scenario, dialogues, production,
    1943.
Monsieur Vincent, scenario (coauthor J. Bernard-Luc)
    and dialogues, 1947.
Anna Karénine, adaptation and dialogues (coauthors
    J. Duvivier and G. Morgan), 1947.
Pattes blanches, scenario (coauthor J. Bernard-Luc), adap-
    tation and dialogues, 1948.
Caroline chérie, adaptation, dialogues, 1950.
Deux Sous de violettes, adaptation and dialogues (co-
    author Monelle Valentin), 1951.
Le Rideau rouge (Ce Soir on joue Macbeth), scenario,
    adaptation, dialogues, 1952.
Un Caprice de Caroline chérie, adaptation, dialogues,
    1952.
Le Chevalier de la nuit, adaptation, dialogues, 1953.

SELECTED BOOKS AND ARTICLES TREATING ANOUILH

Albérès, René-Marill, *La Révolte des écrivains d'aujour-
    d'hui,* Paris, Corrêa, 1949.
Barsacq, André, "A l'Atelier pendant près de quinze ans,"
    *Cahiers de la compagnie Madeleine Renaud—Jean-
    Louis Barrault,* Vol. 26, Paris, Julliard, 1959.
Barsacq, André, and Touchard, Pierre-Aimé, "Roméo et
    Jeannette," *Le Spectateur,* Feb. 11, 1947.

Bishop, Thomas, *Pirandello and the French Theatre,* New York, New York University Press, 1960.

Blanchart, Paul, "Jean Anouilh ou le sauvage," *Théâtre,* No. 3, Paris, Pavois, 1945.

Brasillach, Robert, "Jean Anouilh, ou le Mythe du baptême," *Les Quatre Jeudis,* Paris, Balzac, 1944.

Brée, Germaine, "The Innocent Amusements of Jean Anouilh," *Horizon,* Nov. 1960.

Brooking, Jack, "Jeanne d'Arc, the Trial Notes, and Anouilh," *Theatre Annual, 1959,* Cleveland, Western Reserve University Press, 1960.

Brule, Claude, "Anouilh toujours sauvage," *Opéra,* Jan. 24, 1951.

Carat, Jacques, "Anouilh romantique et giralducien," *Paru,* Nov. 1946.

Champigny, Robert, "Theatre in a Mirror: Anouilh," *Yale French Studies,* Vol. 14, 1954–55.

Chastaing, Maxime, "Jean Anouilh," *Esprit,* March 1947.

Chiari, Joseph, *The Contemporary French Theatre: The Flight from Naturalism,* London, Rockliff, 1958.

Colette, *La Jument noire,* in *Oeuvres complètes,* Vol. 10, Paris, Flammarion, 1949.

Curtis, Anthony, *New Developments in the French Theatre,* London, Curtain Press, 1948.

Didier, Jean, *A la Rencontre de Jean Anouilh,* Brussels, La Sixaine, 1946.

Fowlie, Wallace, *Dionysus in Paris, a Guide to French Contemporary Theatre,* New York, Meridian Books, 1959.

Gignoux, Hubert, *Jean Anouilh,* Paris, Temps Présent, 1946.

Gignoux, Hubert, with Arthur Adamov, Michel Bouquet, and Maurice Clavel, "Jean Anouilh deviendra-t-il un auteur classique?" *Arts,* Oct. 27, 1961.

Grossvogel, David I., *The Self-Conscious Stage in Modern French Theatre,* New York, Columbia University Press, 1958.

Guicharnaud, Jacques, with June Beckelman, *Modern French Theatre from Giraudoux to Beckett*, New Haven, Yale University Press, 1961.

Hobson, Harold, *The French Theatre of Today, an English View*, London, George G. Harrap, 1953.

John, S., "Obsession and Technique in the Plays of Jean Anouilh," *French Studies* (Oxford), April 1957.

Kemp, Robert, *La Vie du théâtre*, Paris, Albin Michel, 1956.

Kushner, Eva, *Le Mythe d'Orphée dans la littérature française contemporaine*, Paris, Nizet, 1961.

Laurent, Jacques, "L'Agnelle noire" (a parody of Anouilh), *La Table ronde*, Nov. 1951.

Lestienne, Voldemar, "La Grande Fille de Monsieur Anouilh," *Elle*, Nov. 6, 1959.

Luppé, Robert de, *Jean Anouilh*, Paris, Editions Universitaires, 1959.

———, "Jean Anouilh," *Les Nouvelles littéraires*, March 29, 1962.

Malclès, Jean-Denis, "Avec Jean Anouilh," *Cahiers de la Compagnie Madeleine Renaud—Jean-Louis Barrault*, Vol. 26, Paris, Julliard, 1959.

Marcel, Gabriel, *L'Heure théâtrale*, Paris, Plon, 1959.

———, "Le Tragique chez Jean Anouilh," *Revue de Paris*, June 1949.

Marsh, Edward Owen, *Jean Anouilh, Poet of Pierrot and Pantaloon*, London, W. H. Allen, 1953.

Nelson, Robert, *Play within a Play*, New Haven, Yale University Press, 1958.

Neveux, Georges, "Une Pièce noire peinte en rose," *Arts*, Jan. 25, 1952.

Piétri, Roland, "Avec Jean Anouilh," *Cahiers de la Compagnie Madeleine Renaud—Jean-Louis Barrault*, Vol. 26, Paris, Julliard, 1959.

Poujol, Jacques, "Tendresse et cruauté dans le théâtre de Jean Anouilh," *French Review*, April 1952.

Pronko, Leonard Cabell, *The World of Jean Anouilh,*
Berkeley, University of California Press, 1961.

Radine, Serge, *Anouilh, Lenormand, Salacrou: Trois
Dramaturges à la recherche de leur vérité,* Geneva,
Trois Collines, 1951.

Les Sept, "Anouilh ou le rose et le noir," *La Gazette des
lettres,* Dec. 1950.

Index